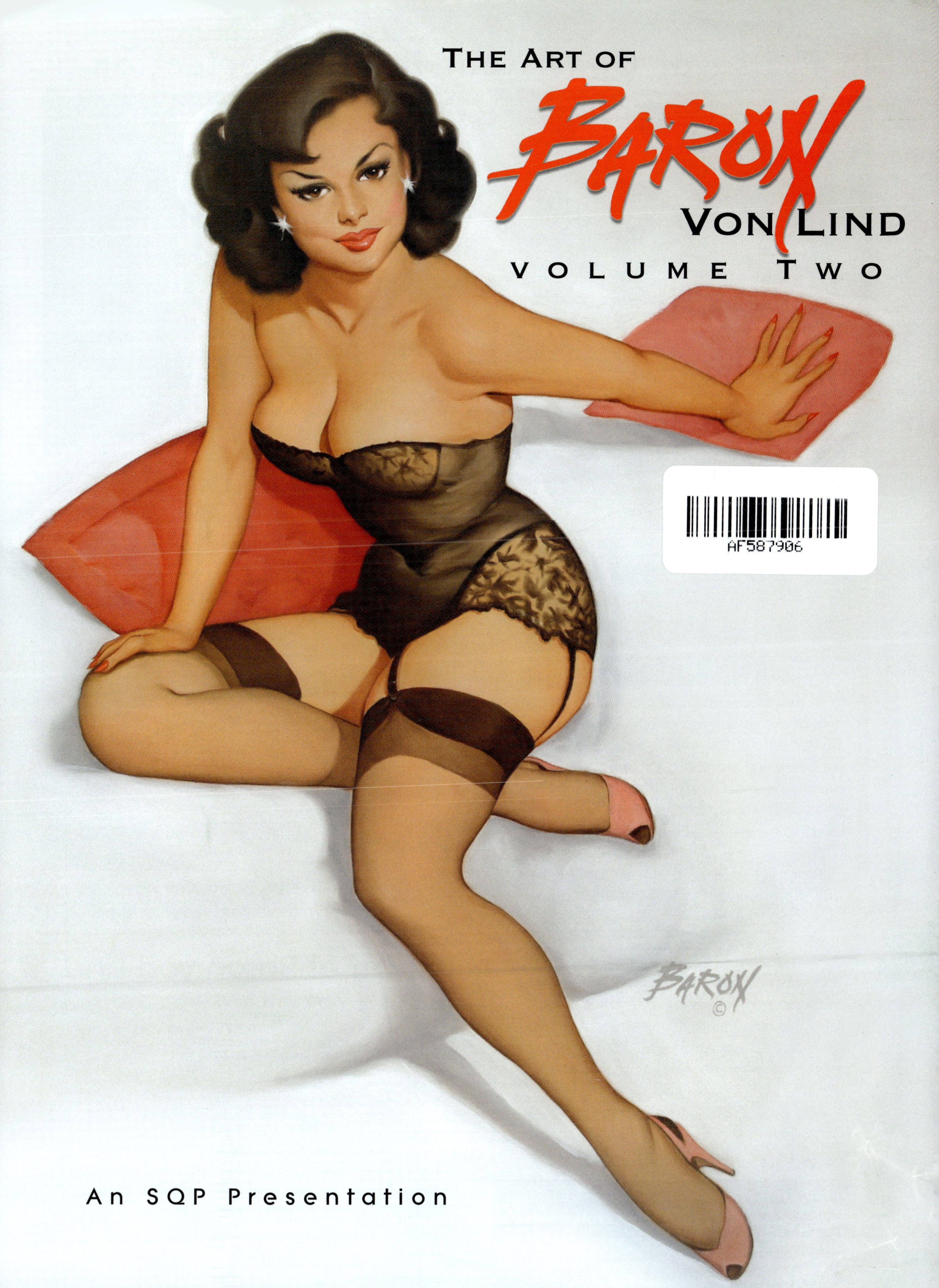
THE ART OF
BARON
VON LIND
VOLUME TWO
AF587906
BARON ©
An SQP Presentation

# In Praise of Consistent Pin-Up Perfection...

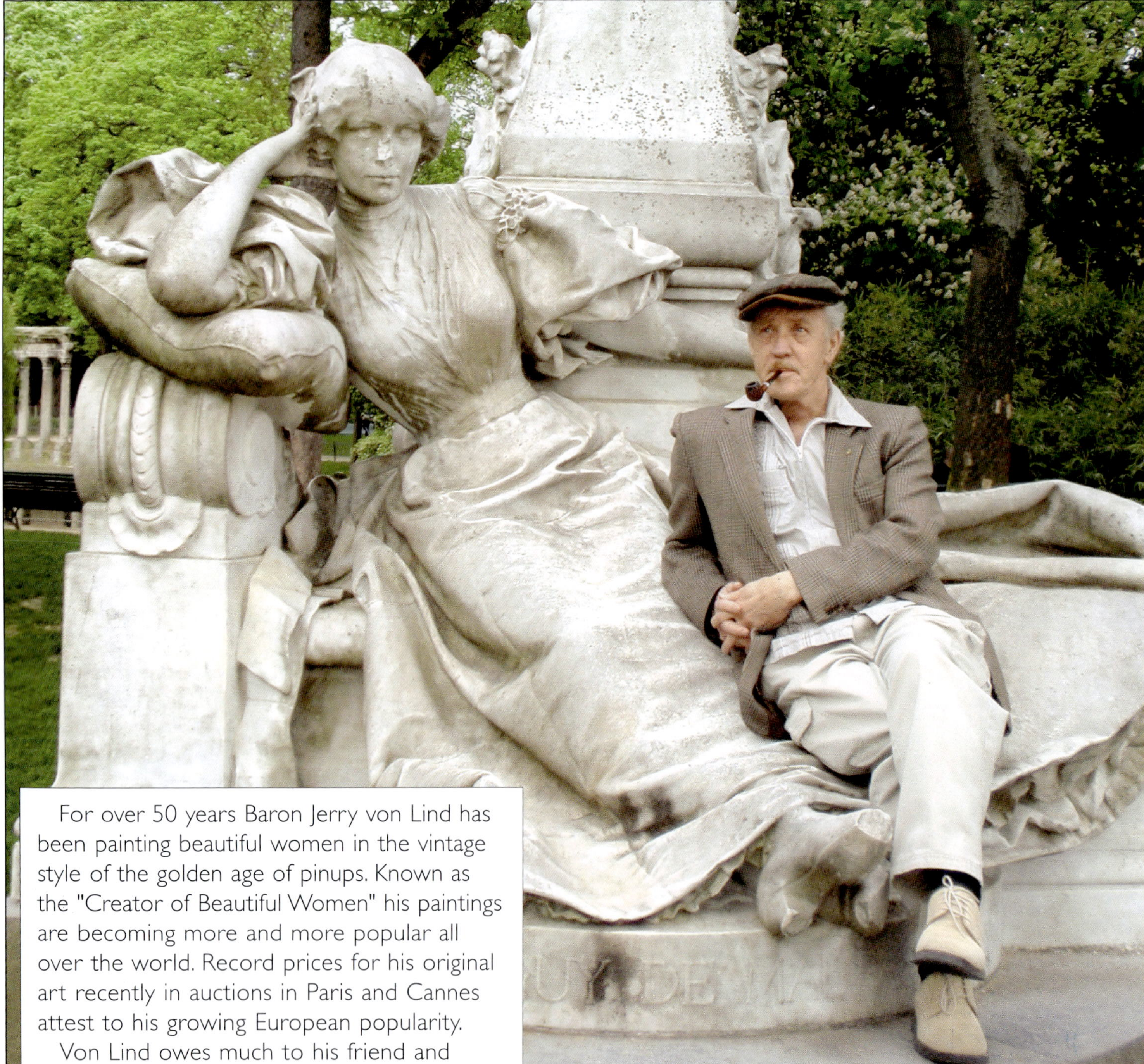

On his latest trip to Paris, Baron took in the sites and sat quite comfortably in the lap of lovely!

For over 50 years Baron Jerry von Lind has been painting beautiful women in the vintage style of the golden age of pinups. Known as the "Creator of Beautiful Women" his paintings are becoming more and more popular all over the world. Record prices for his original art recently in auctions in Paris and Cannes attest to his growing European popularity.

Von Lind owes much to his friend and mentor, Gil Elvgren and others from his days with the Brown & Bigelow calendar company back in St. Paul, Minnesota where Jerry is originally from.

His pinups depict that bygone era of the "American girl next door" that was so popular and is now enjoying such resurgence in the retro market today. That sexy smile and ideal-girl-look that every man would "take home to meet mother" is the very essence of what Baron's pinup art is all about.

Jerry is still creating those beauties in his Florida home and his many fans all over the world inspire him to continue to this day.

**For the latest works of Baron, go to: www.baronvonlind.com**

## The Art of Baron von Lind

### Volume Two

 Printed in China.
Book design by Grassy Knoll Studios.

Published by
SQP Inc.
PO Box 248 - Columbus, NJ 08022

Sal Quartuccio & Bob Keenan - Publishers

For a free full color catalog showcasing the entire SQP line of erotic, fantasy, and pin-up artwork, go to: www.sqpartbooks.com

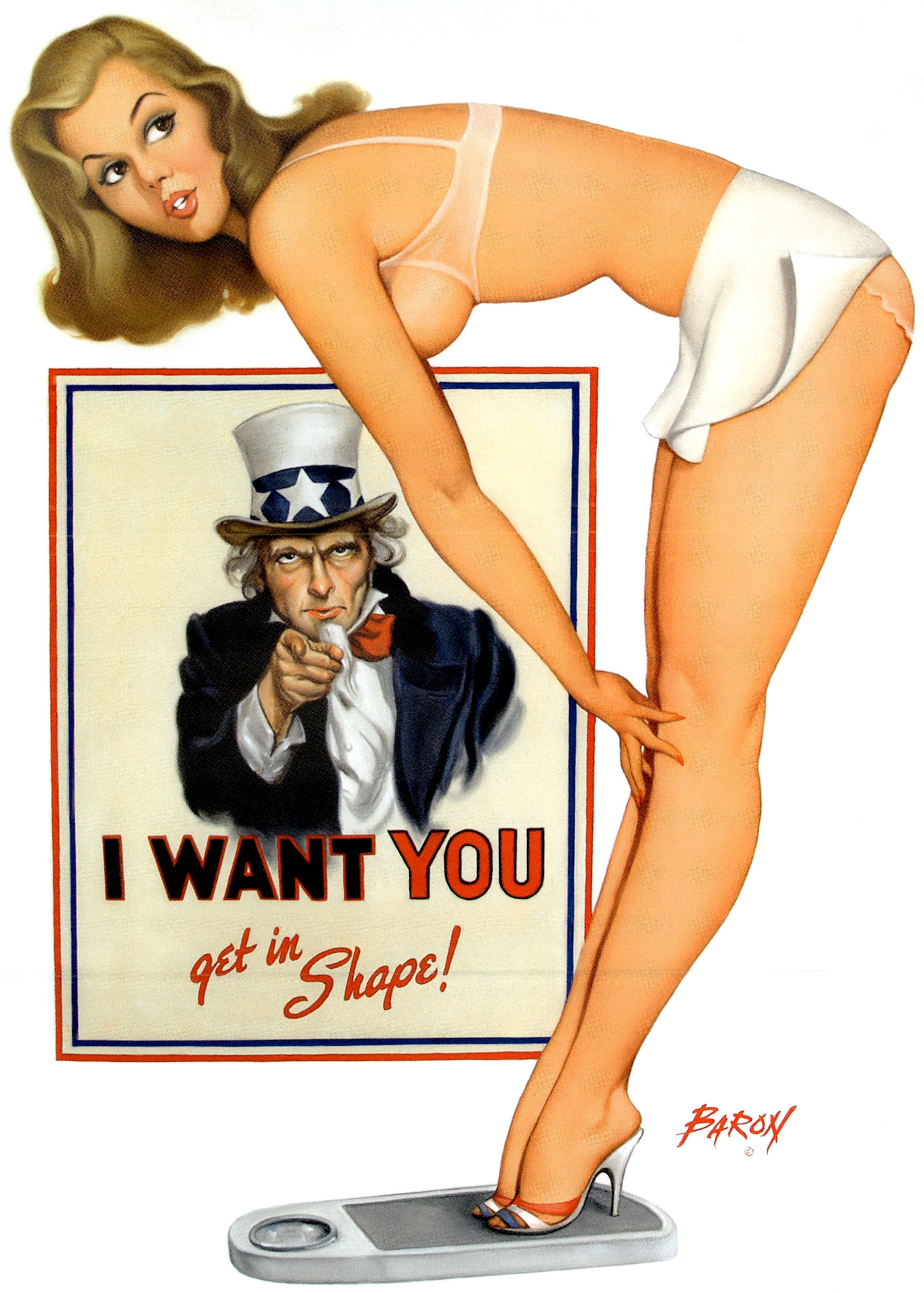
I WANT YOU
get in Shape!
BARON
©

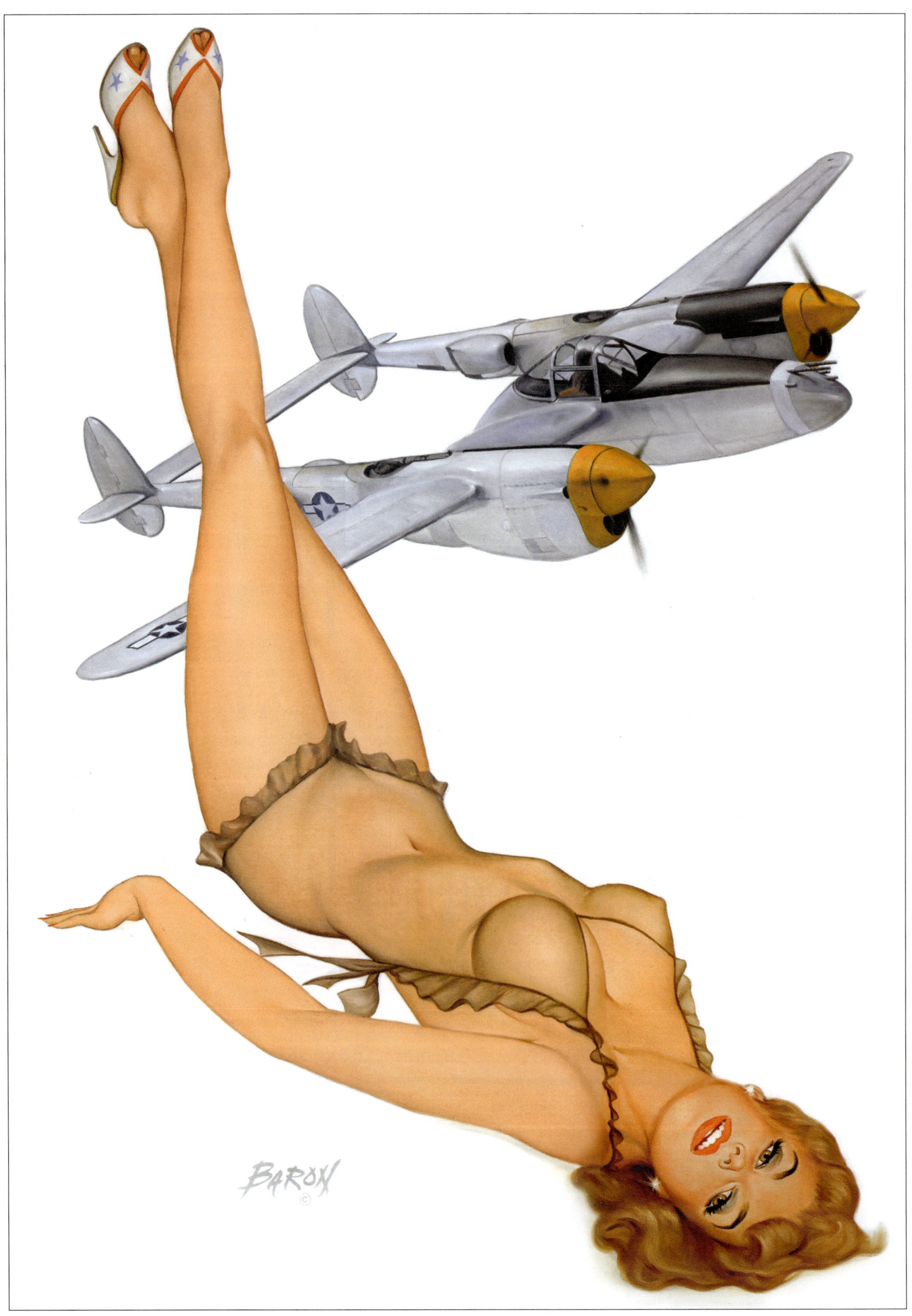
BARON
©

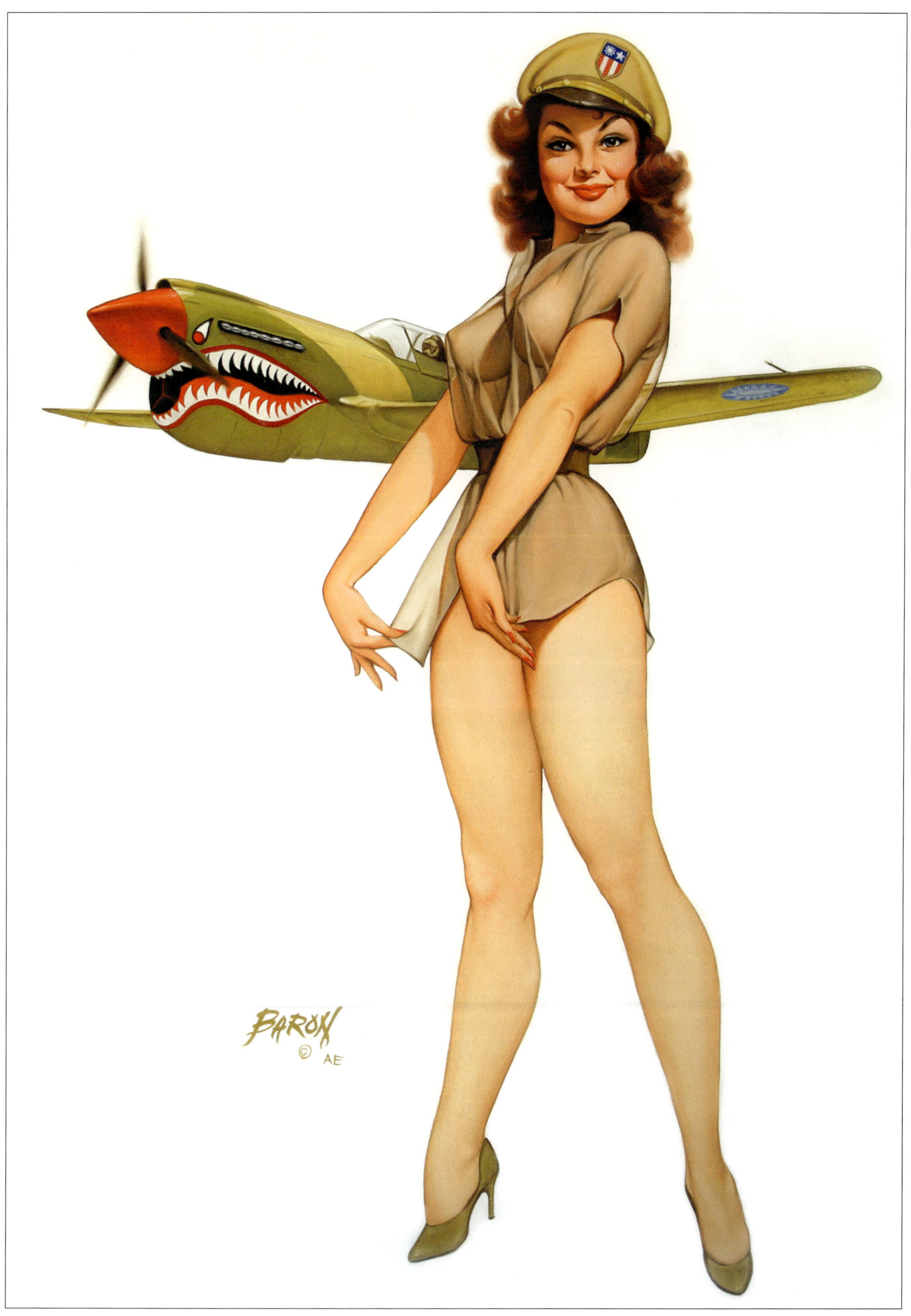
BARON
© AE

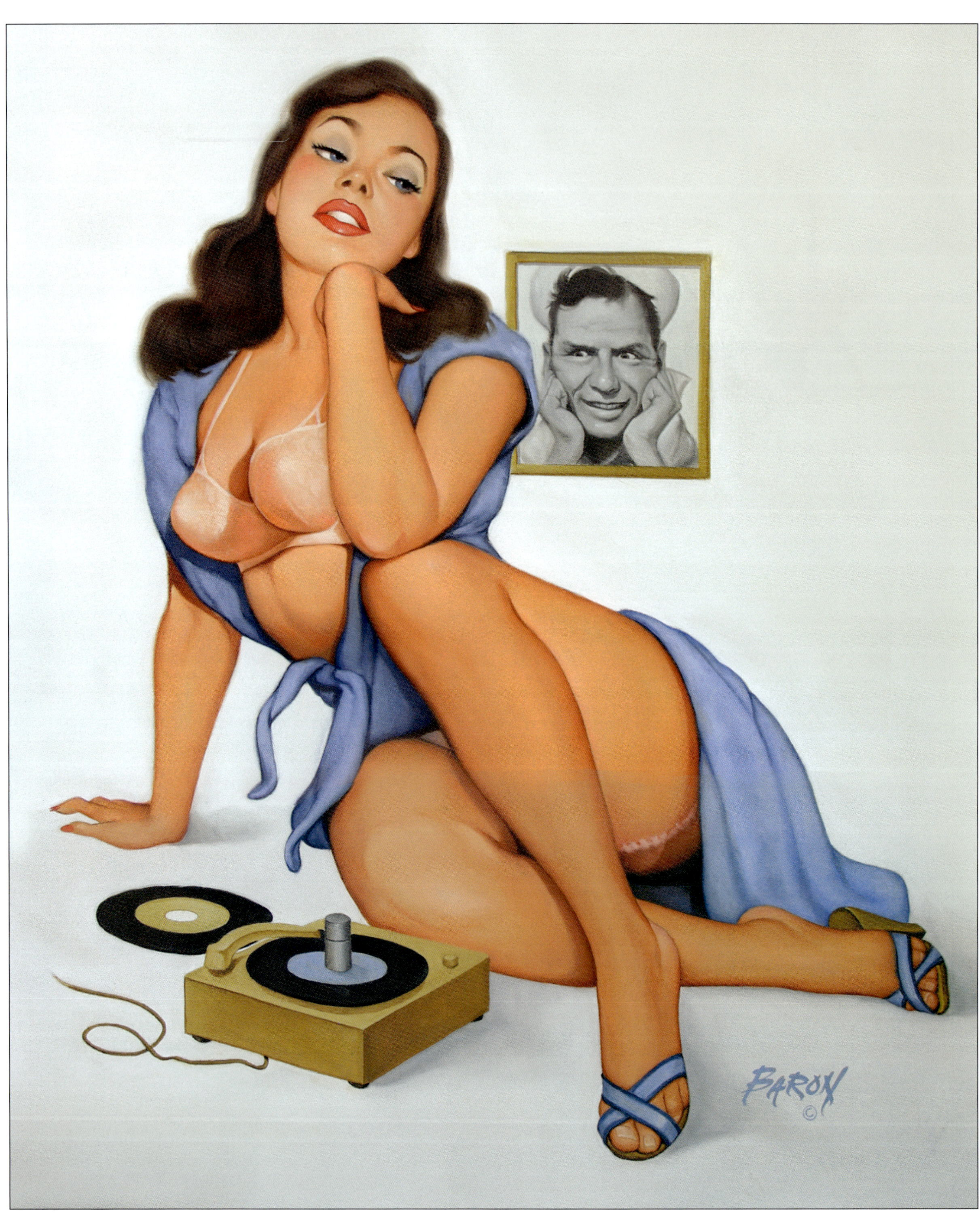
BARON
©

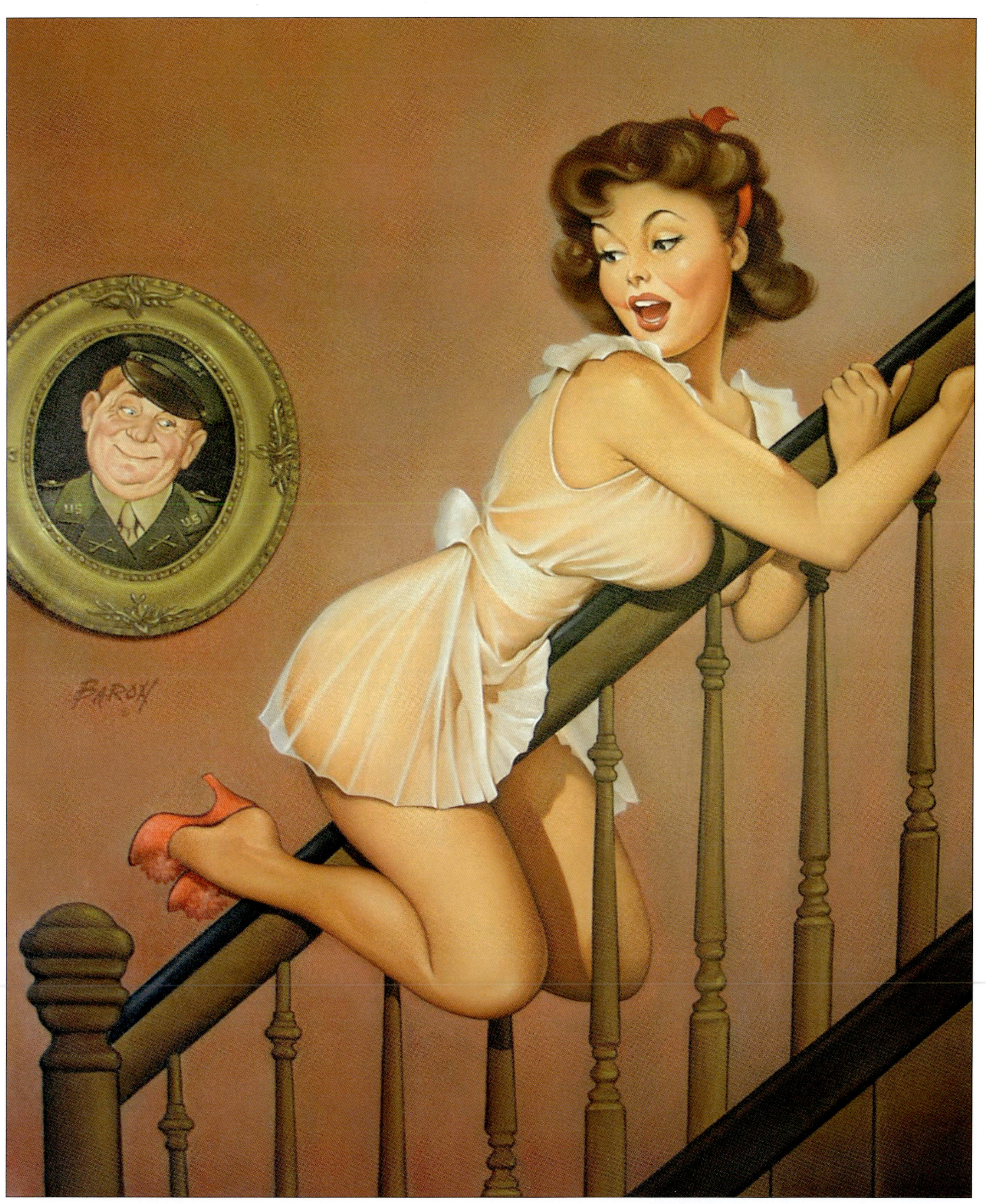
BARON

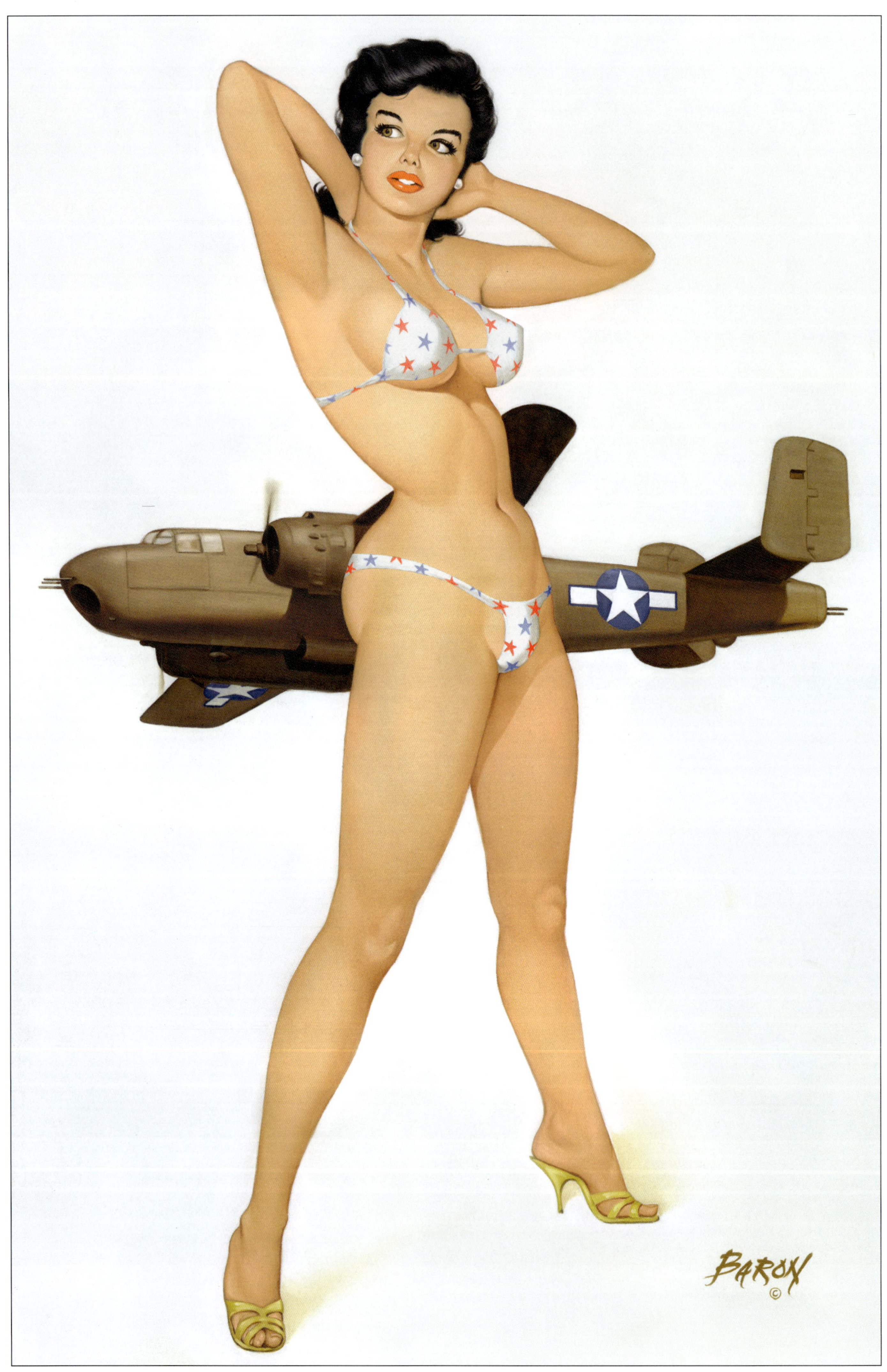
BARON
©

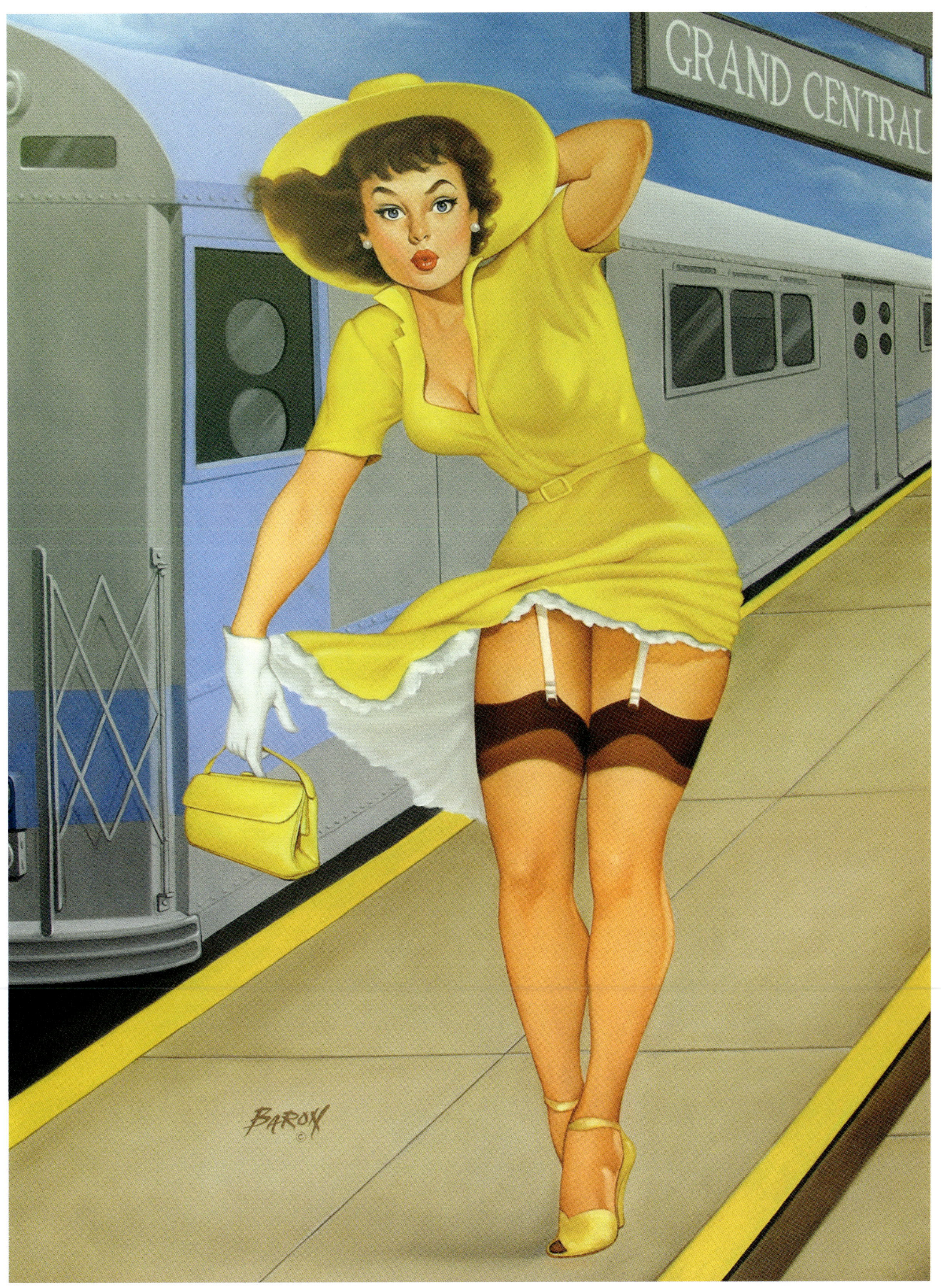
GRAND CENTRAL
BARON

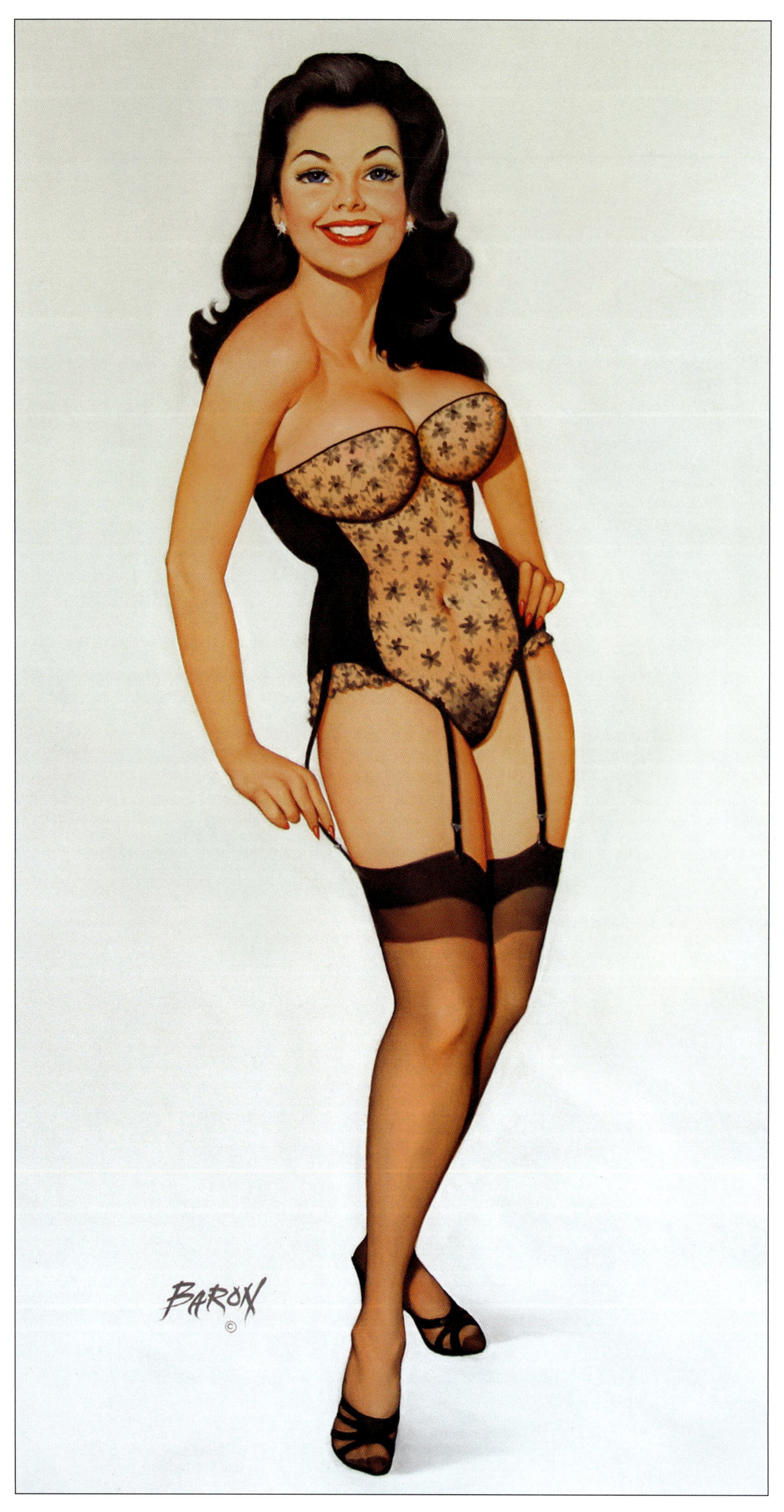
BARON
©

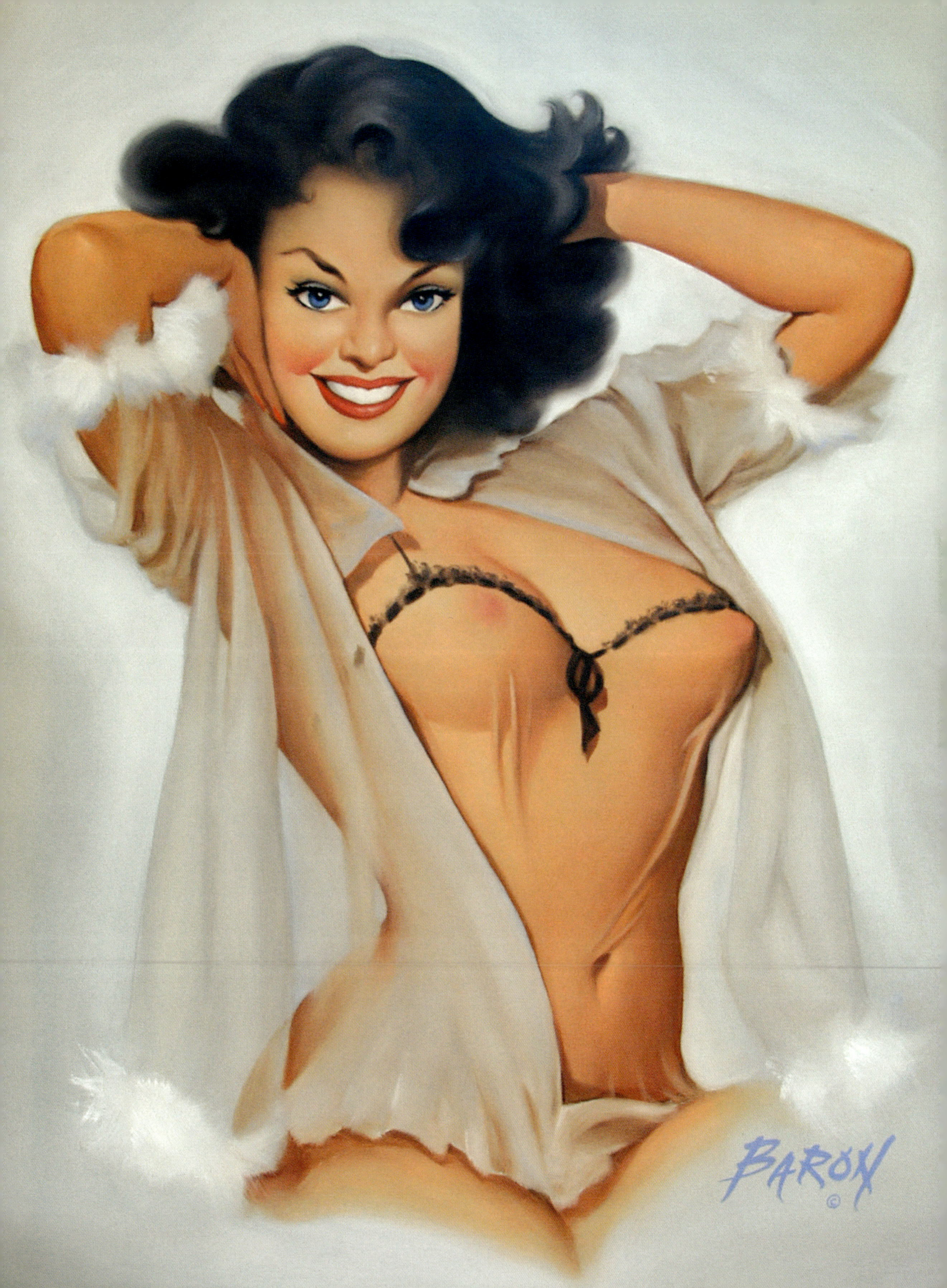
BARON
©

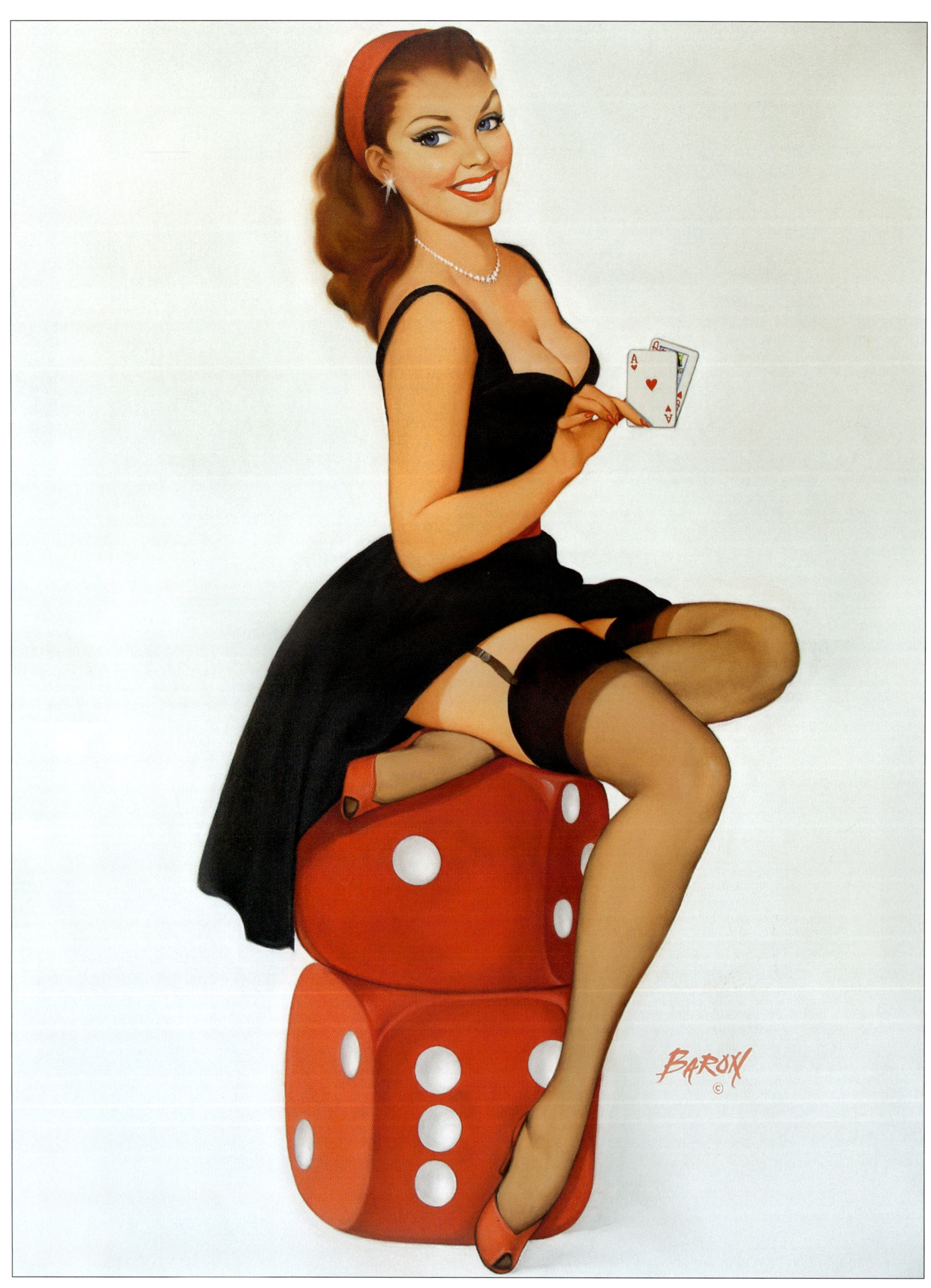
BARON
©

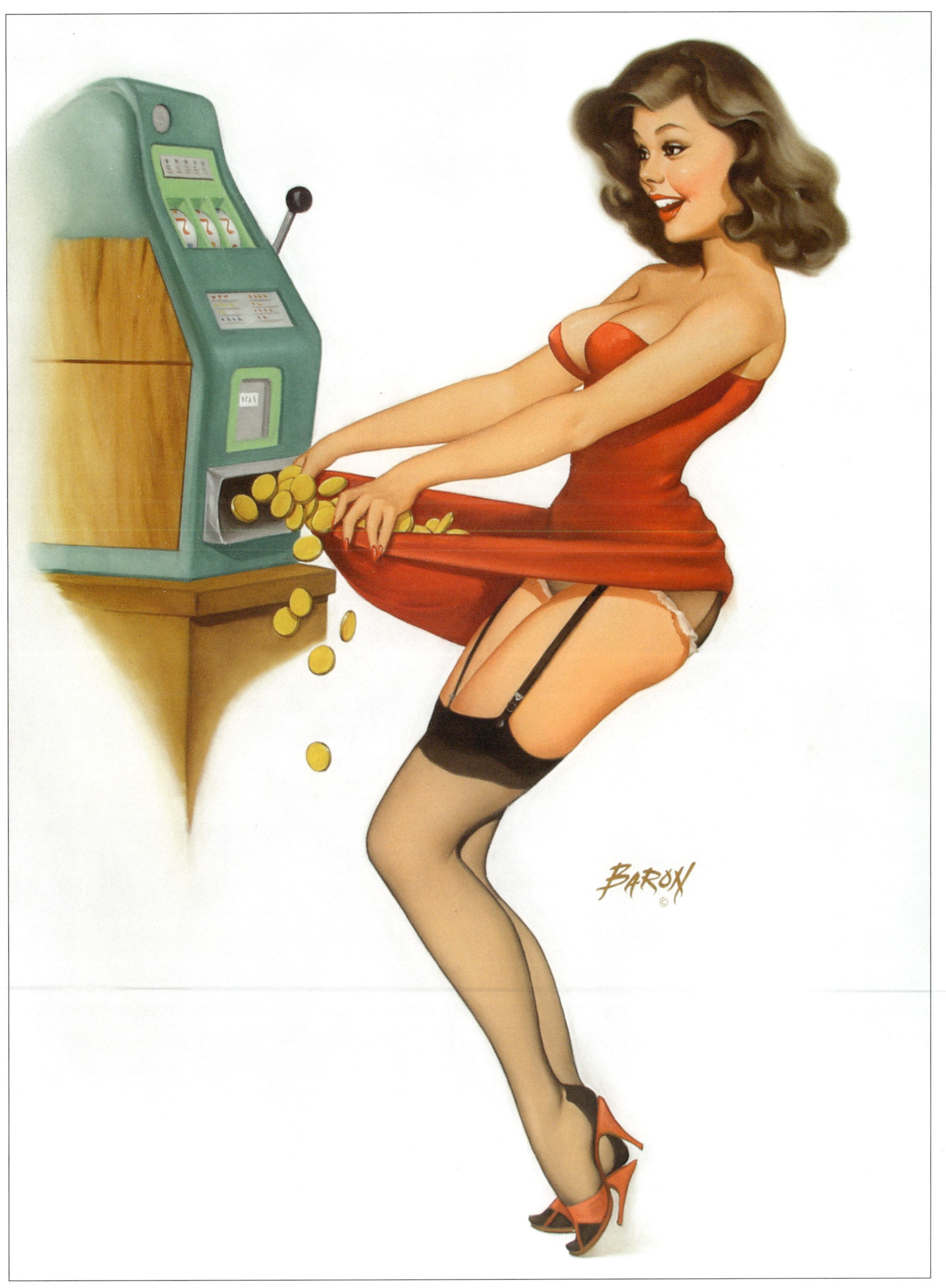
BARON
©

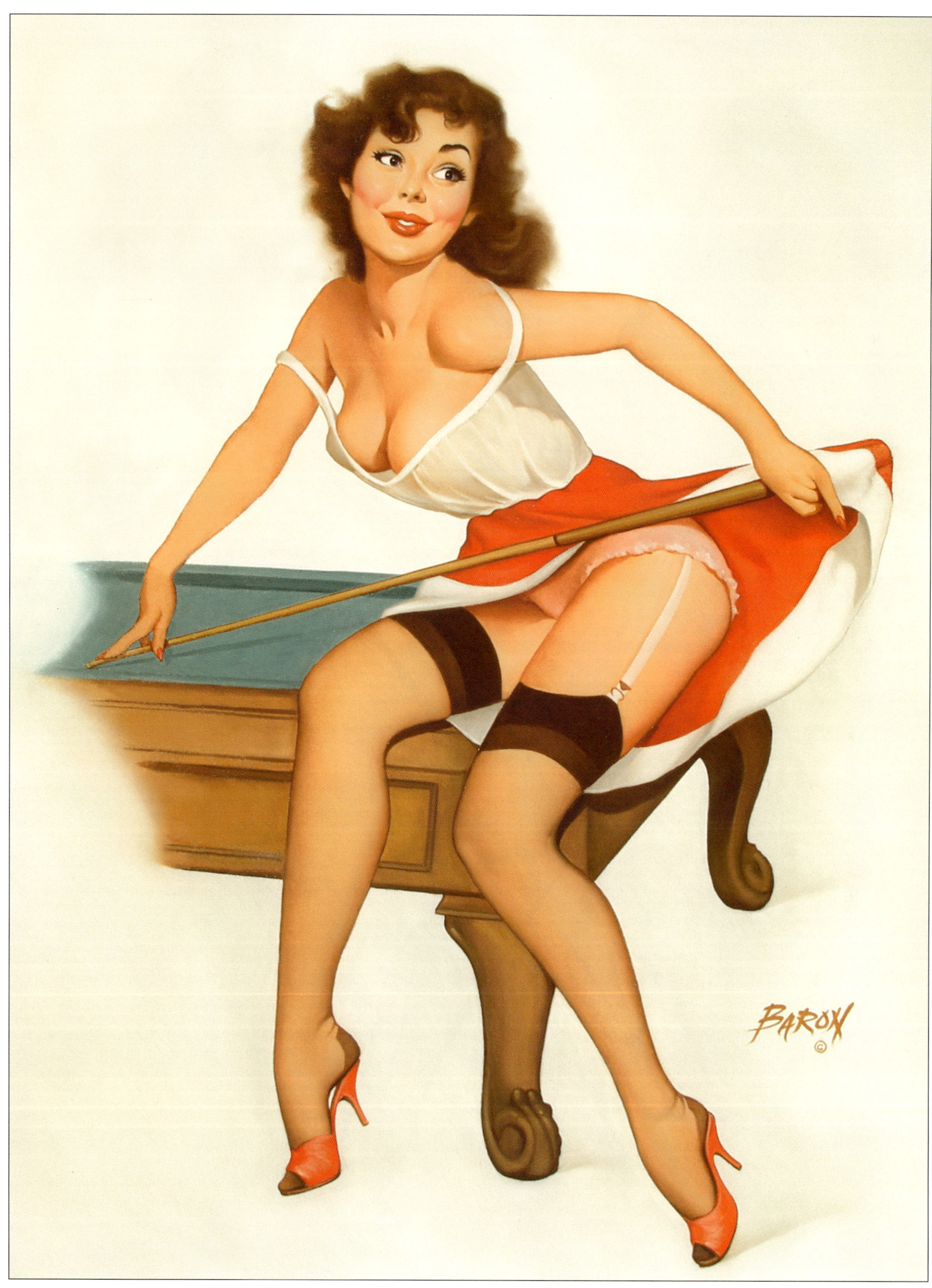
BARON ©

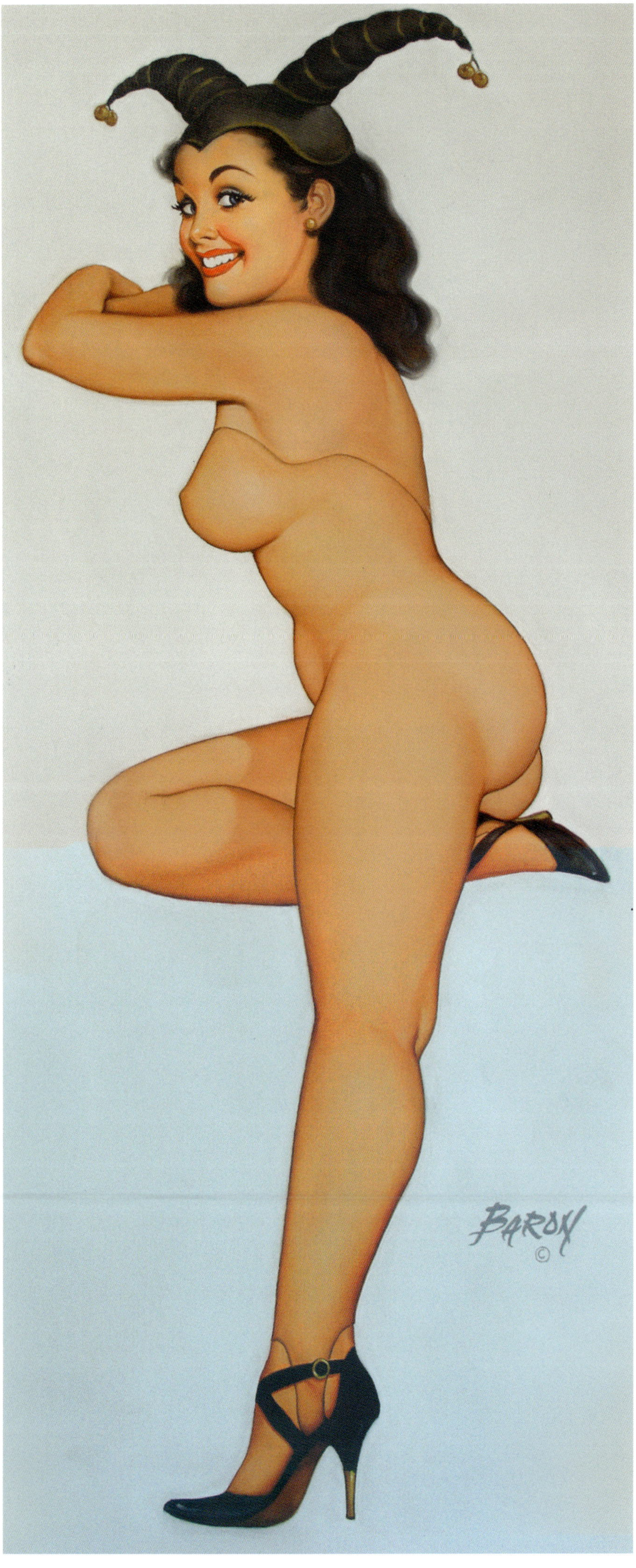

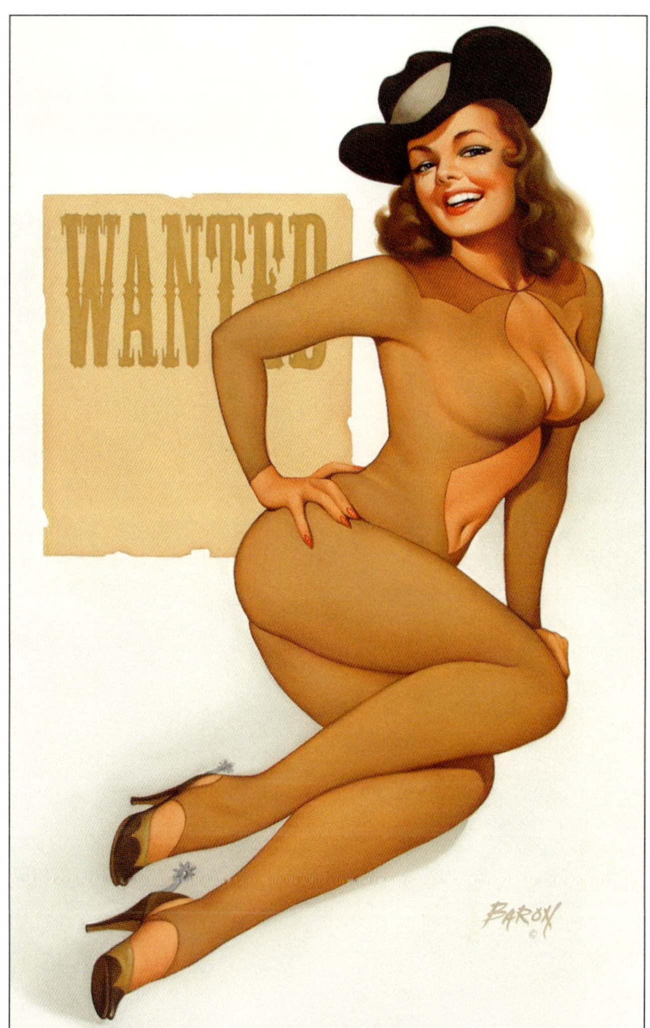
WANTED
BARON

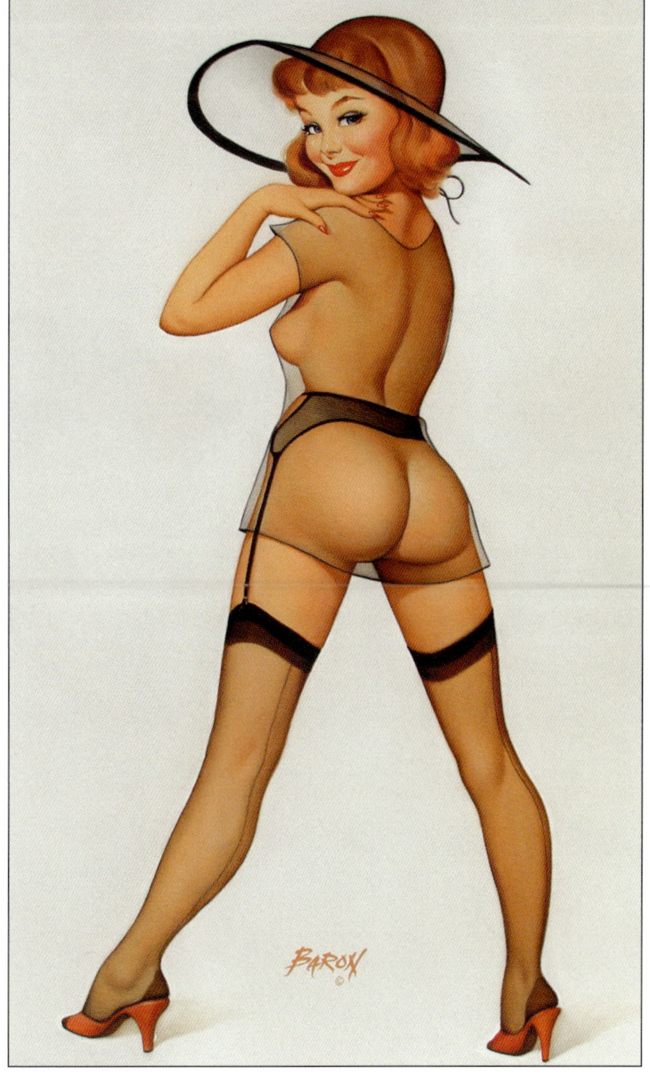
BARON

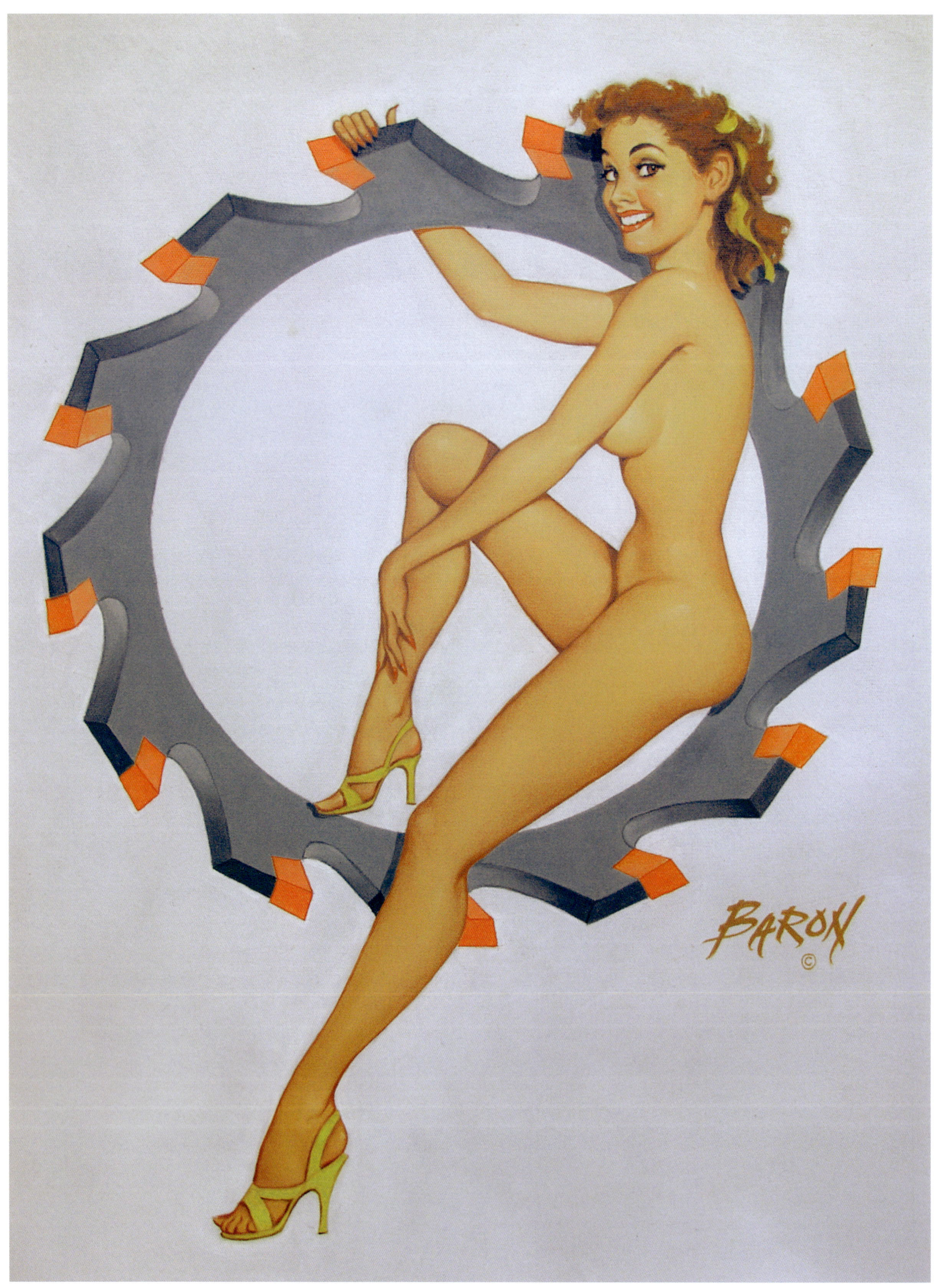
BARON
©

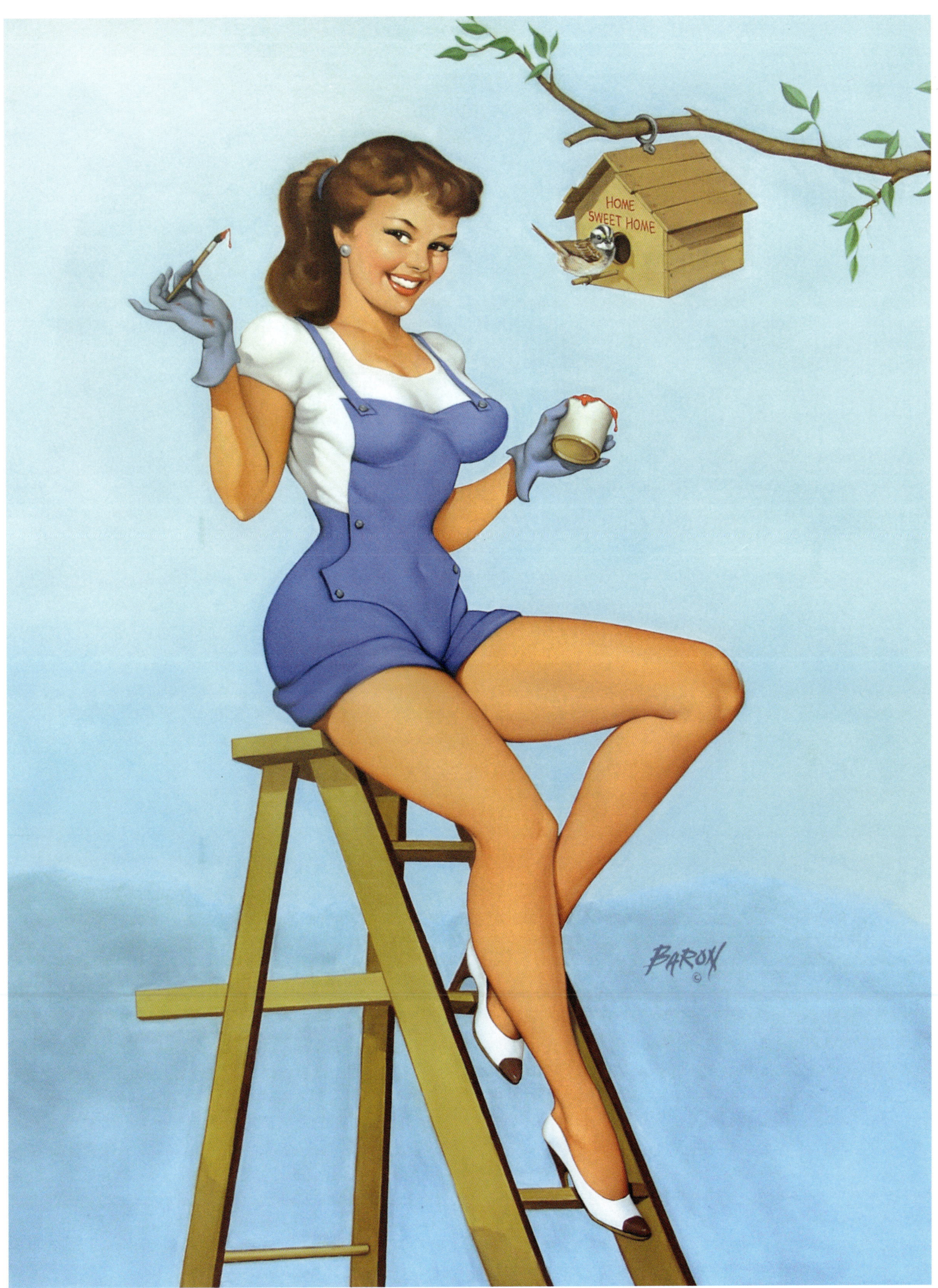
HOME
SWEET HOME
BARON
©

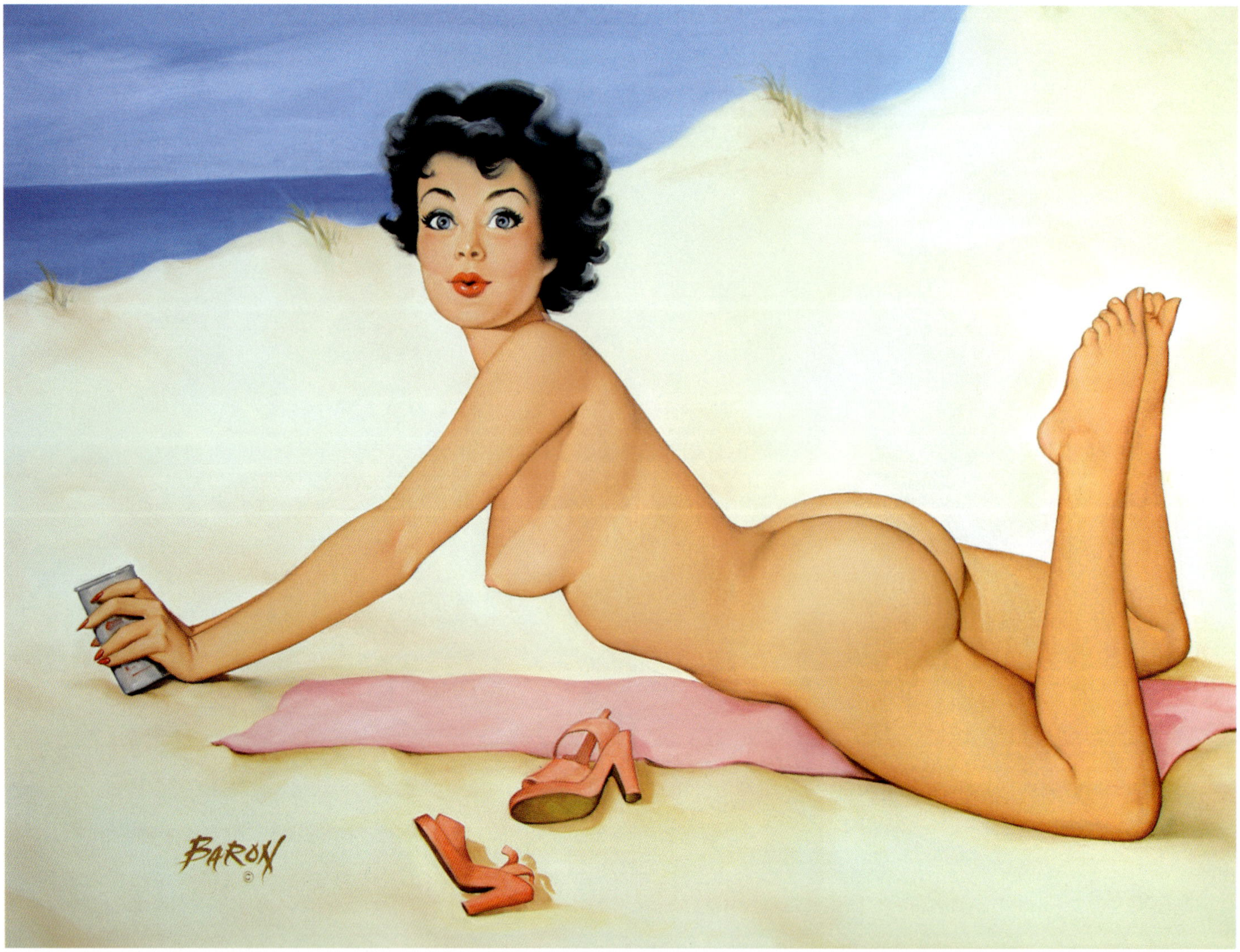

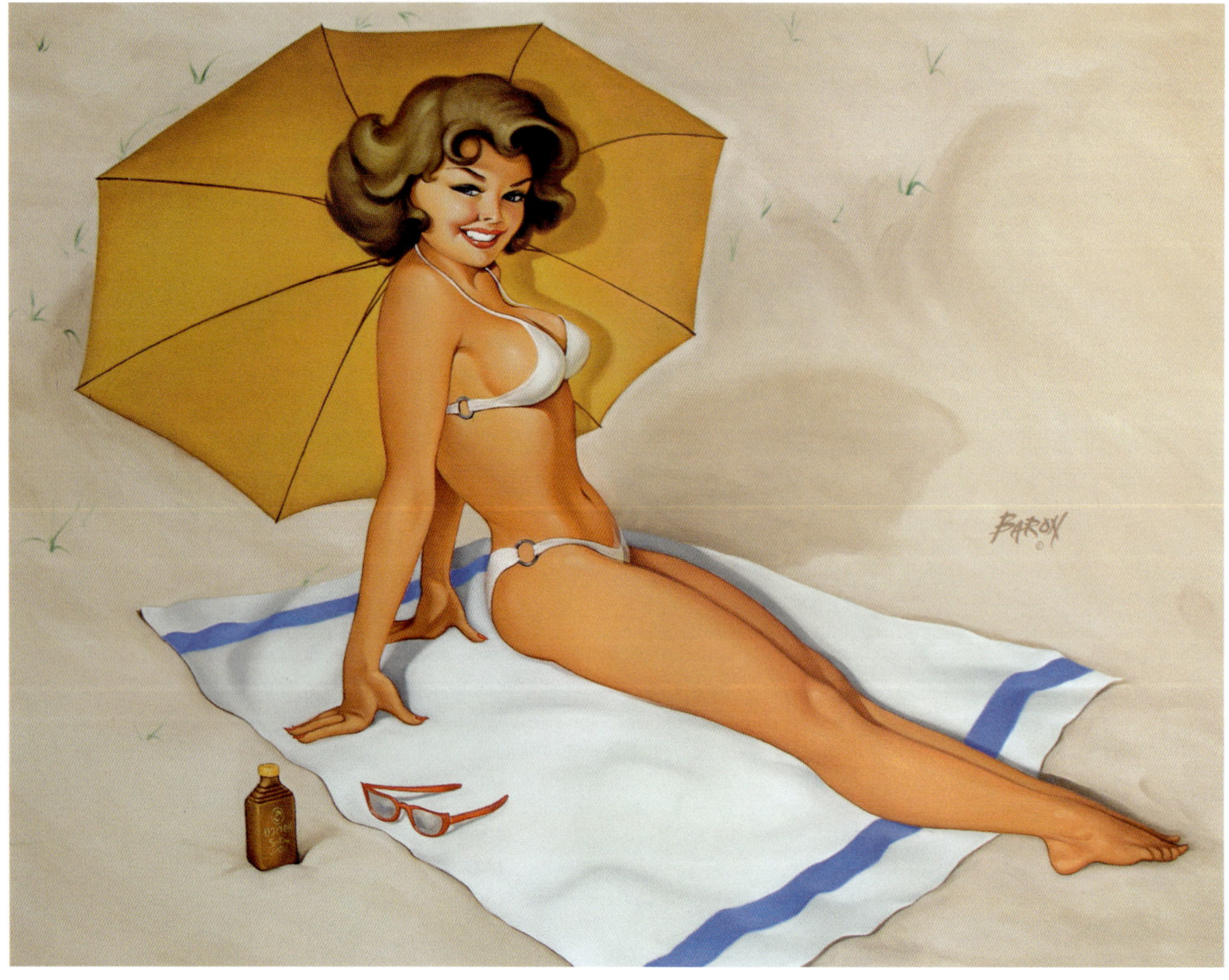
BARON

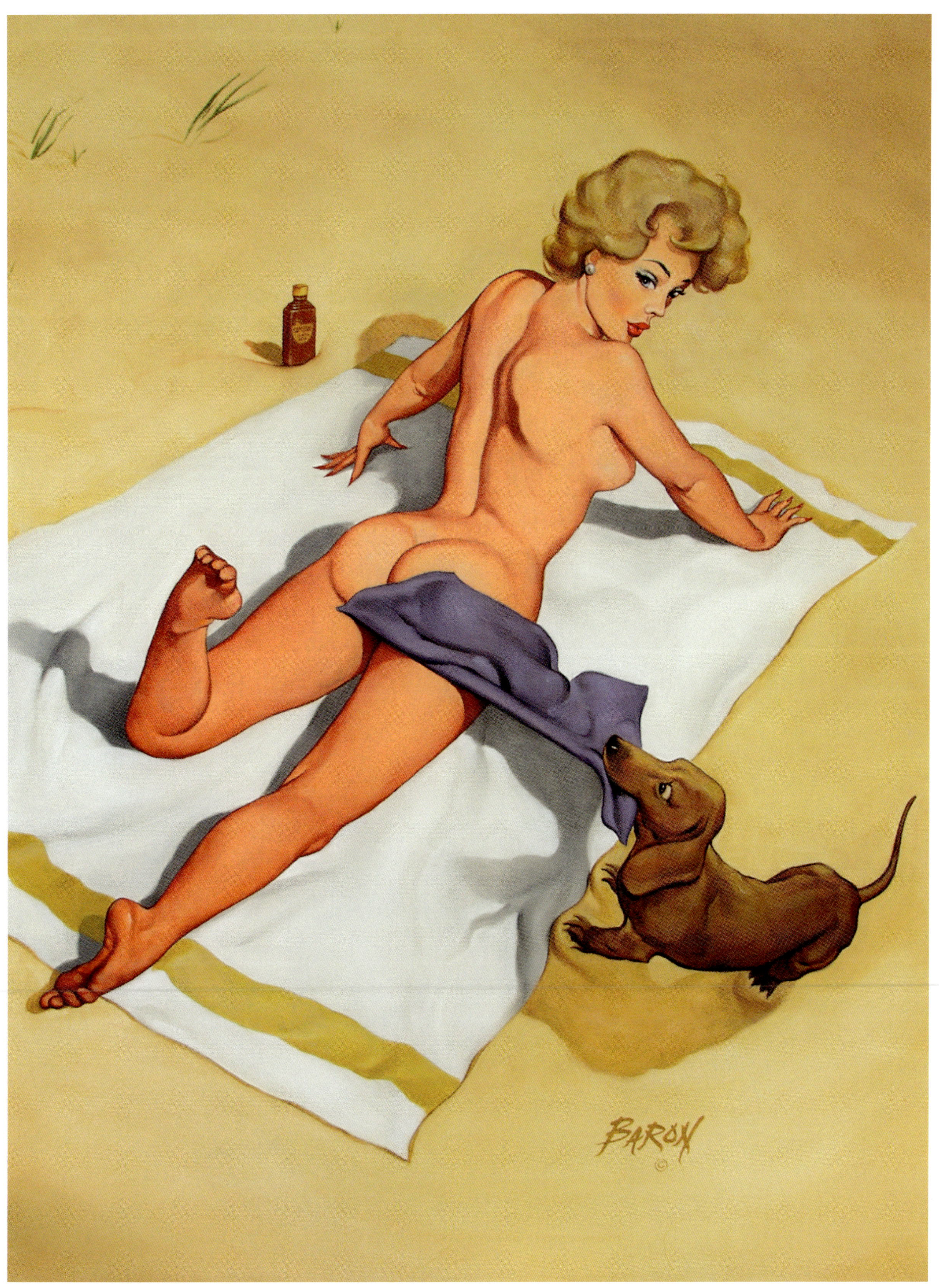
BARON
©

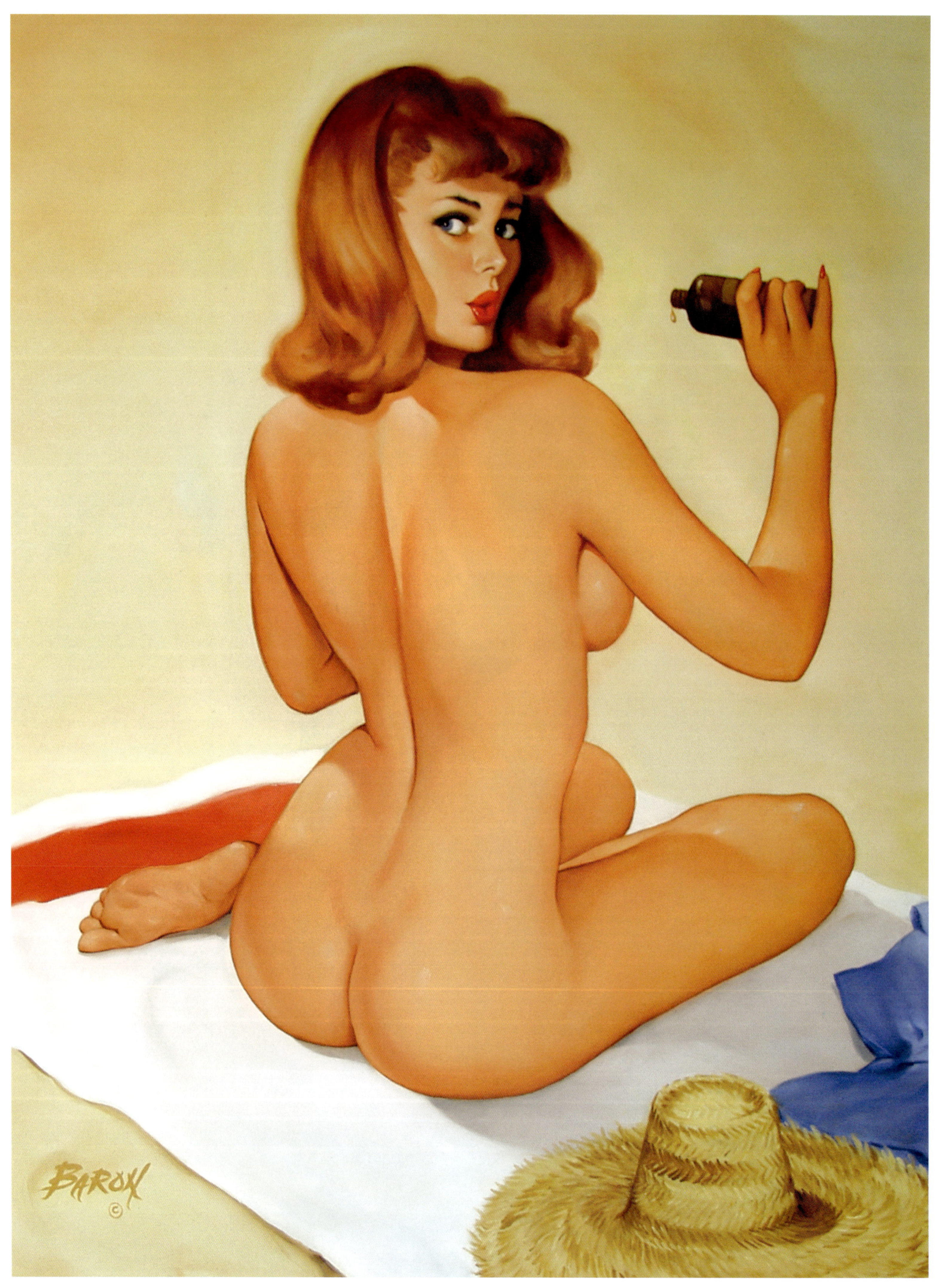
BARON
©

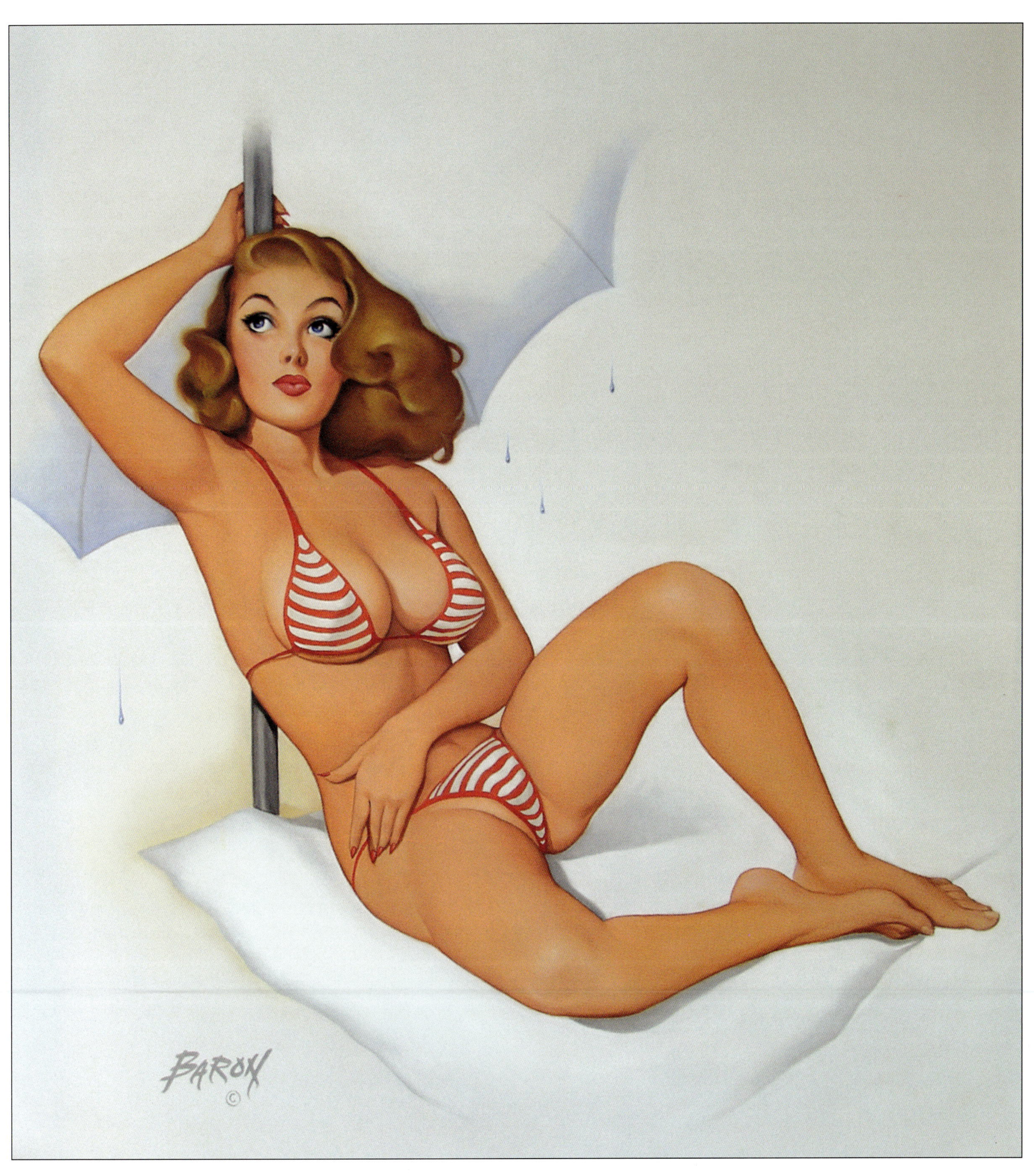
BARON
©

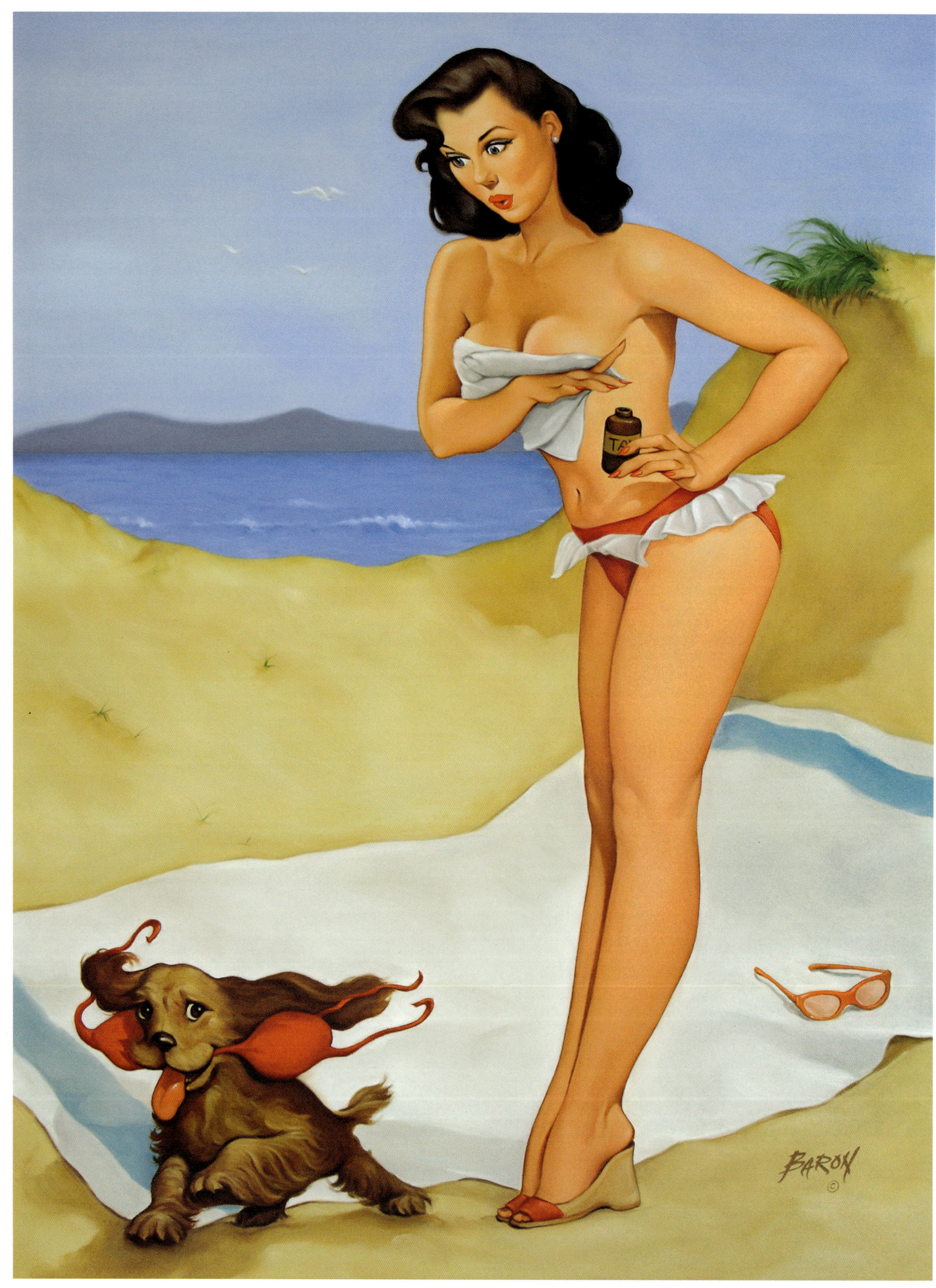
TA
BARON
©

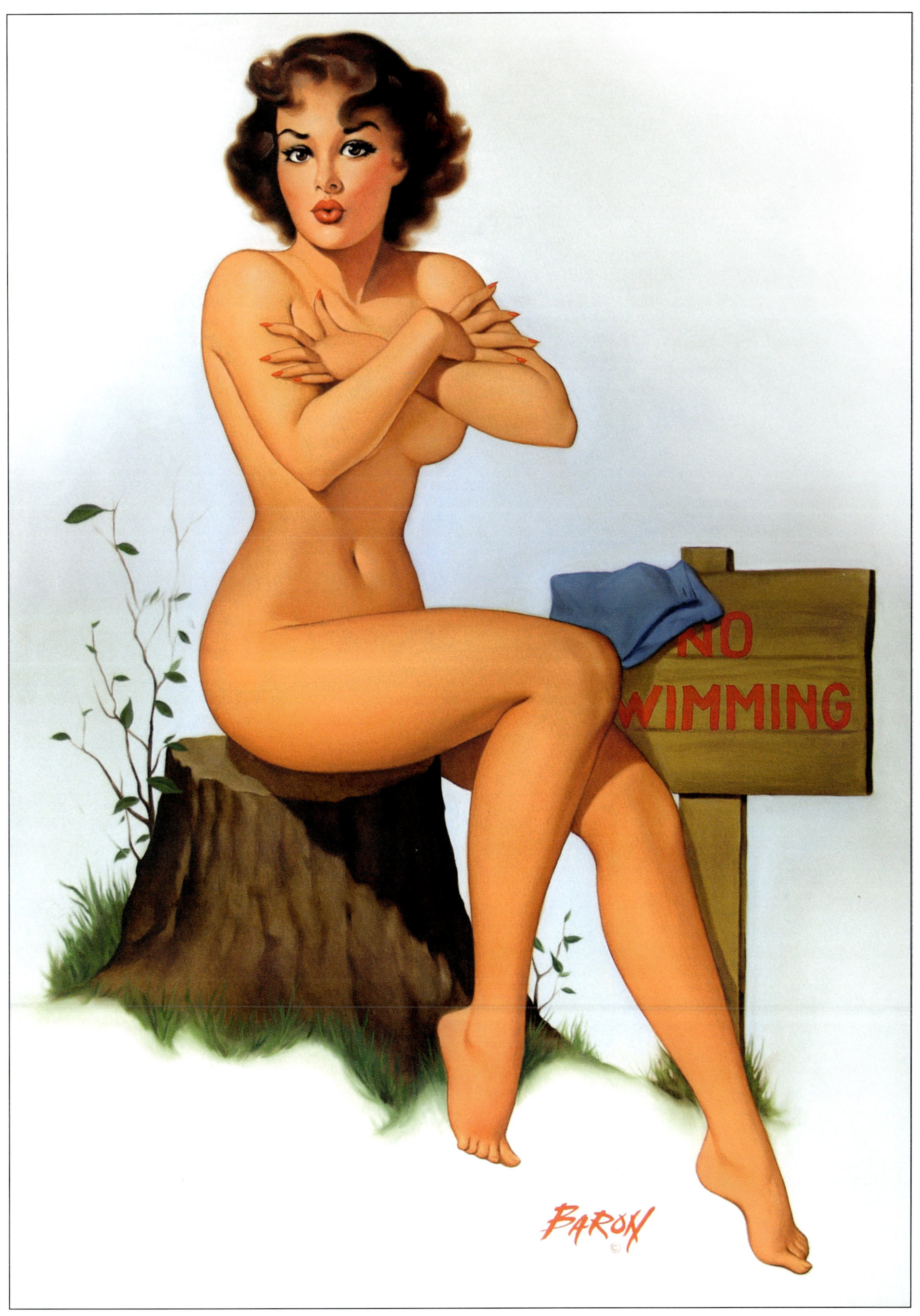
NO
WIMMING
BARON

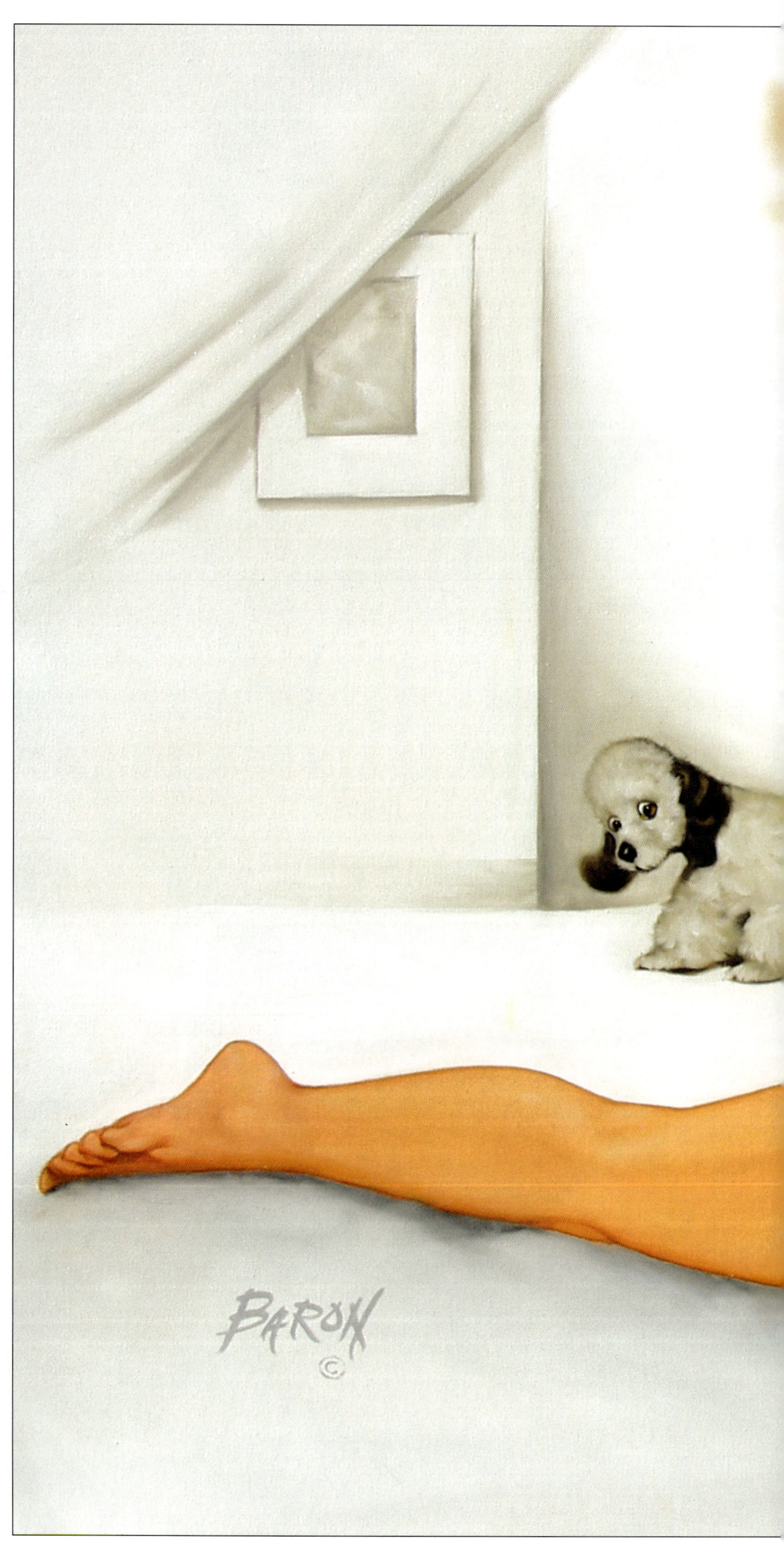
BARON
©

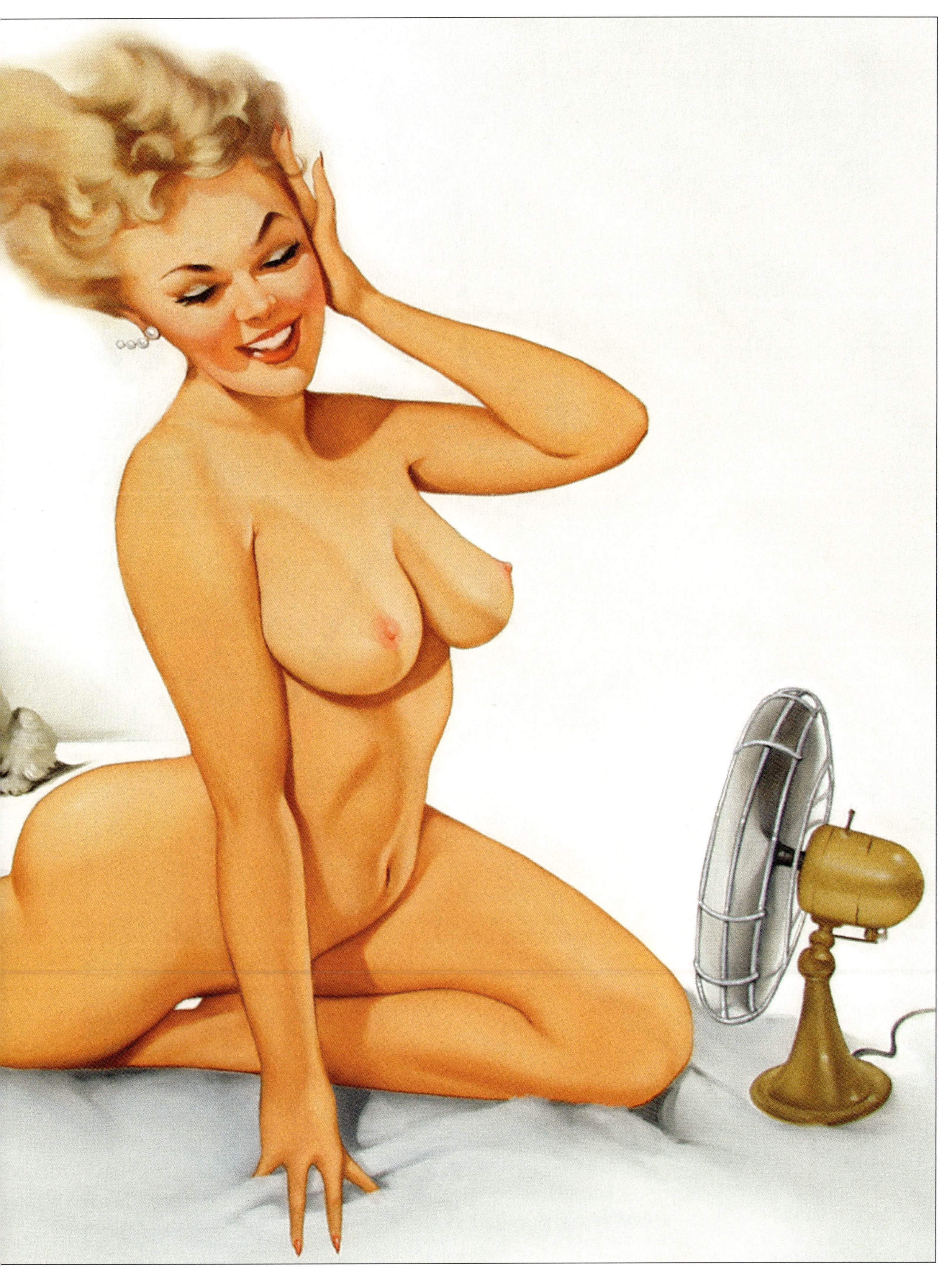

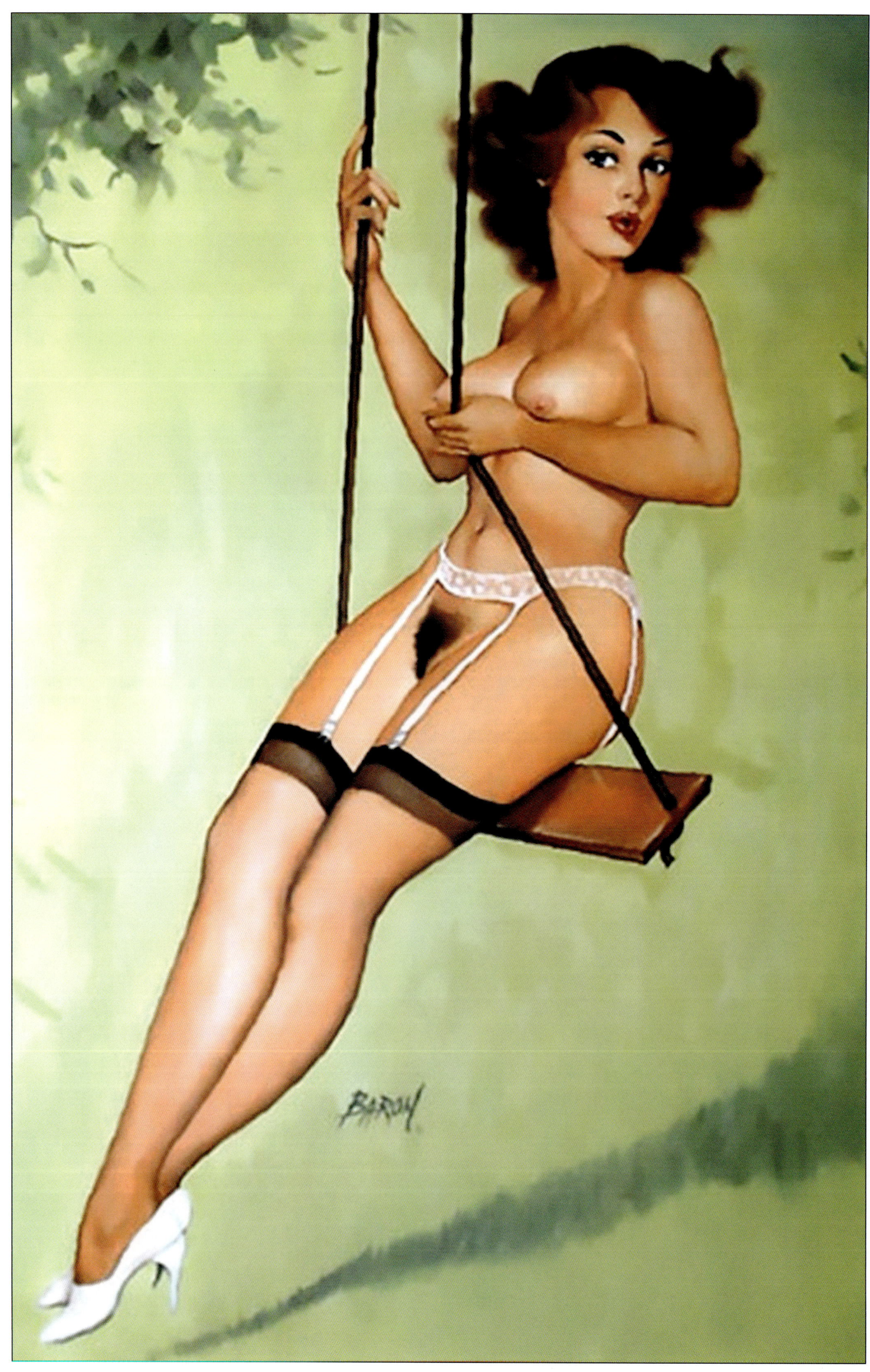
BARON

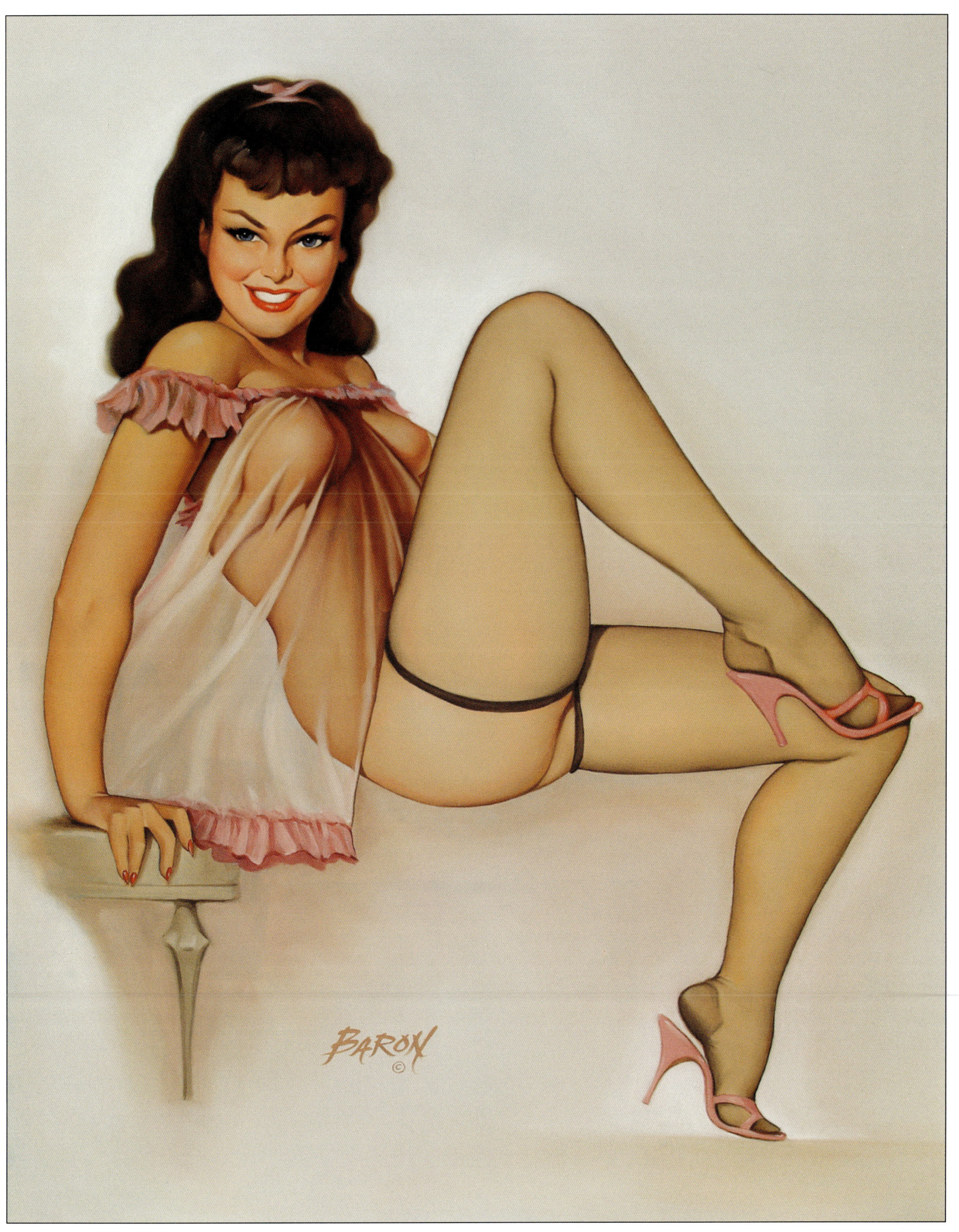
BARON
©

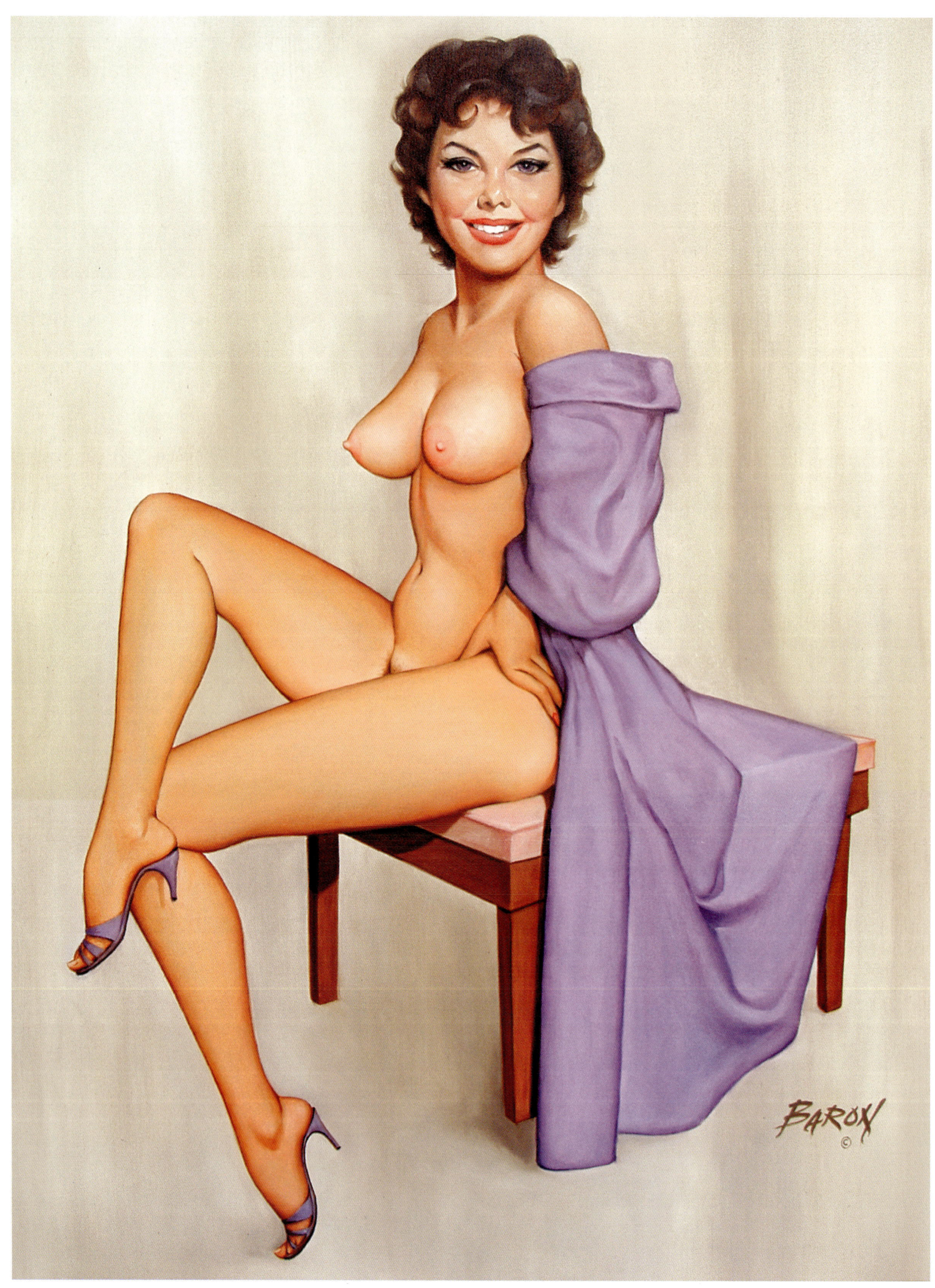
BARON
©

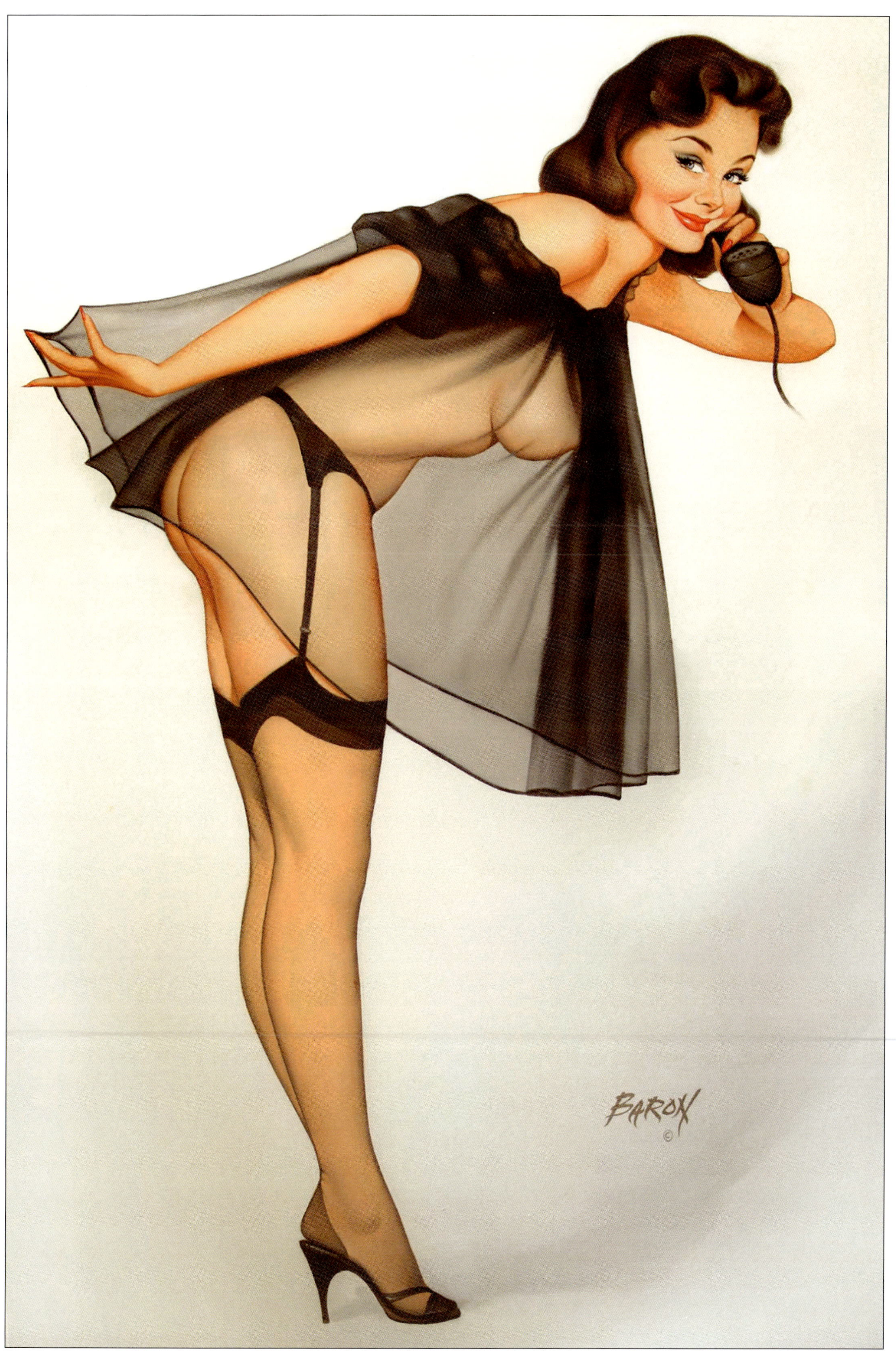
BARON
©

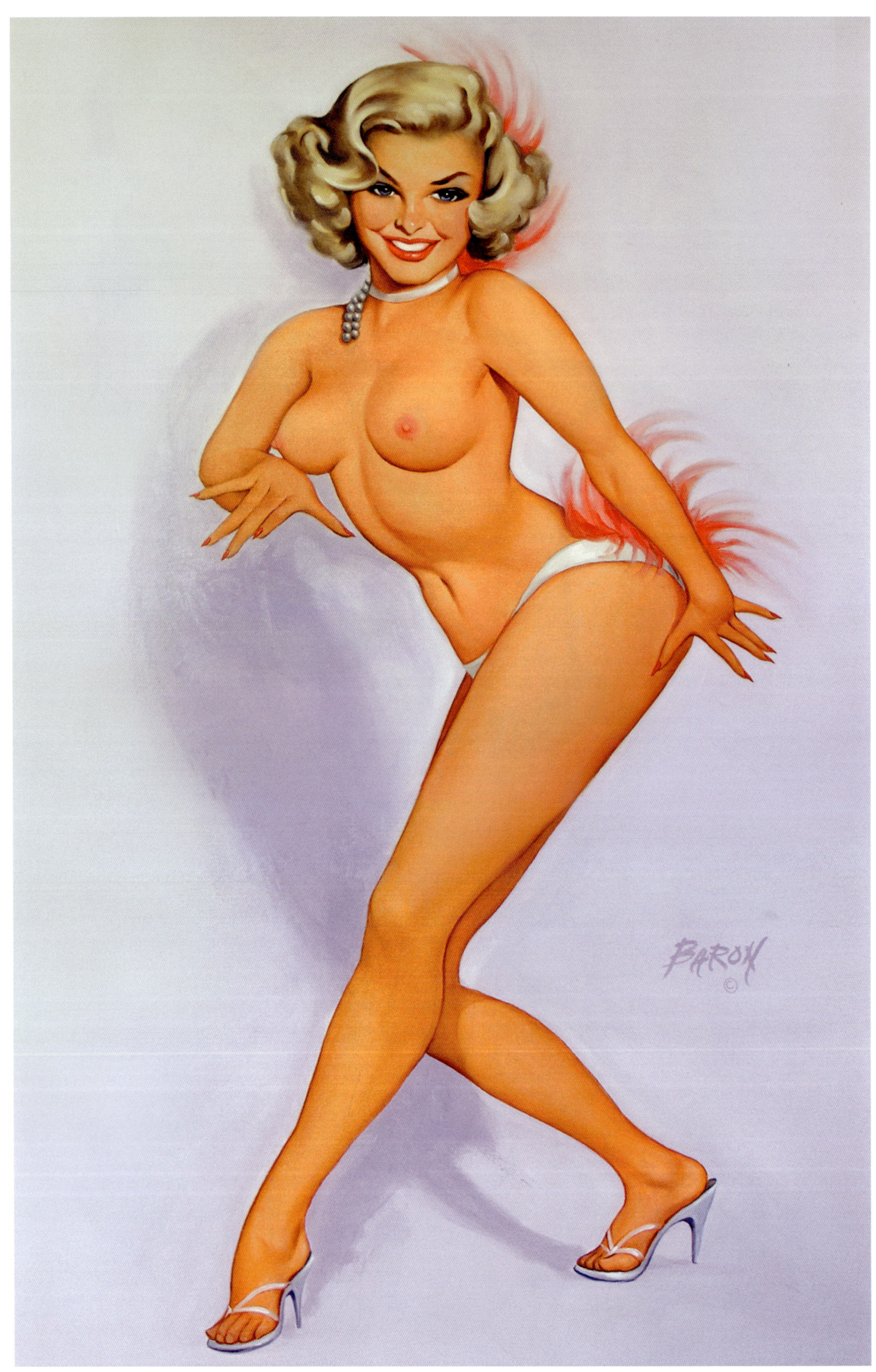
BARON
©

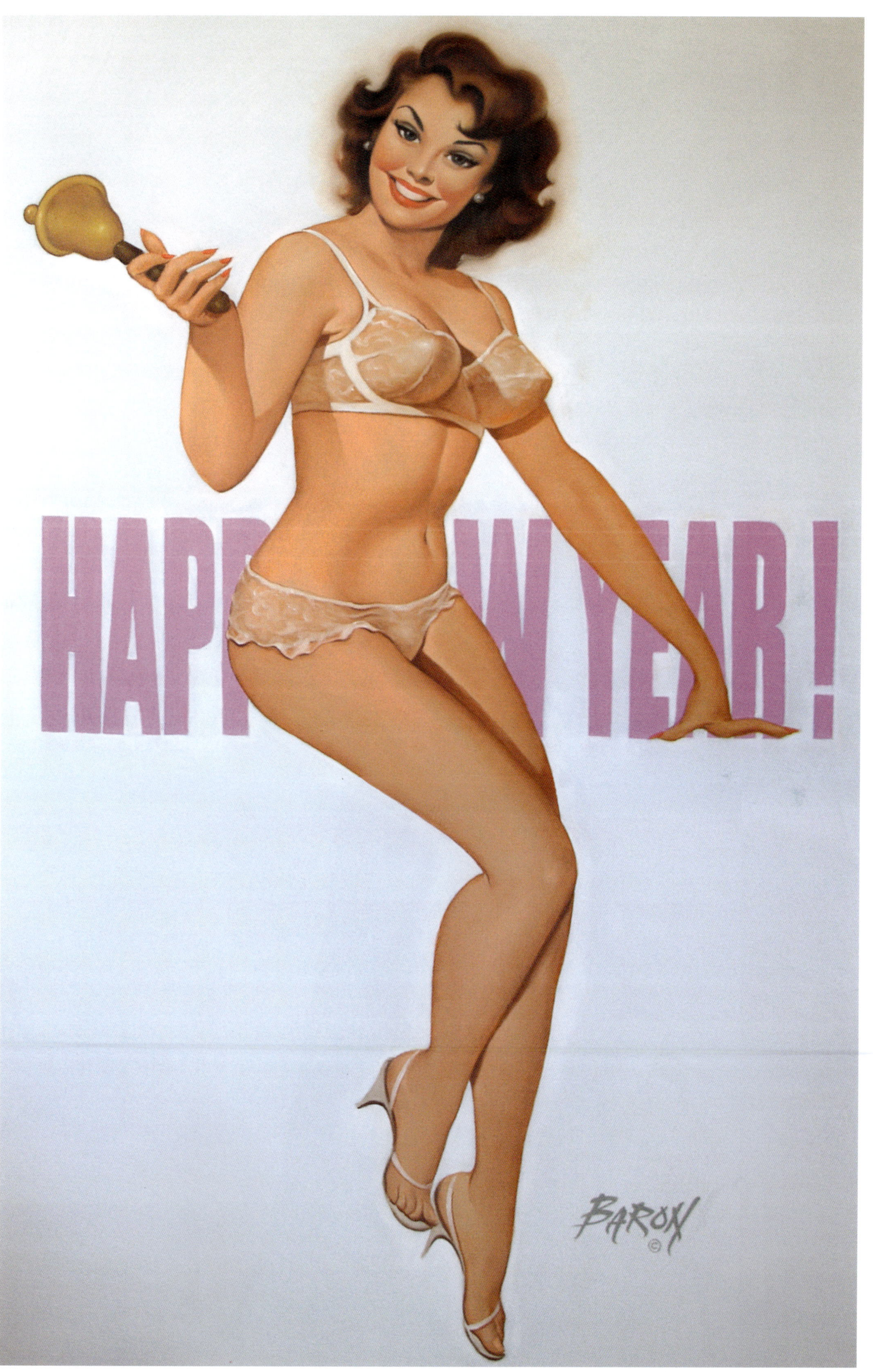
HAPP
W YEAR !
BARON ©

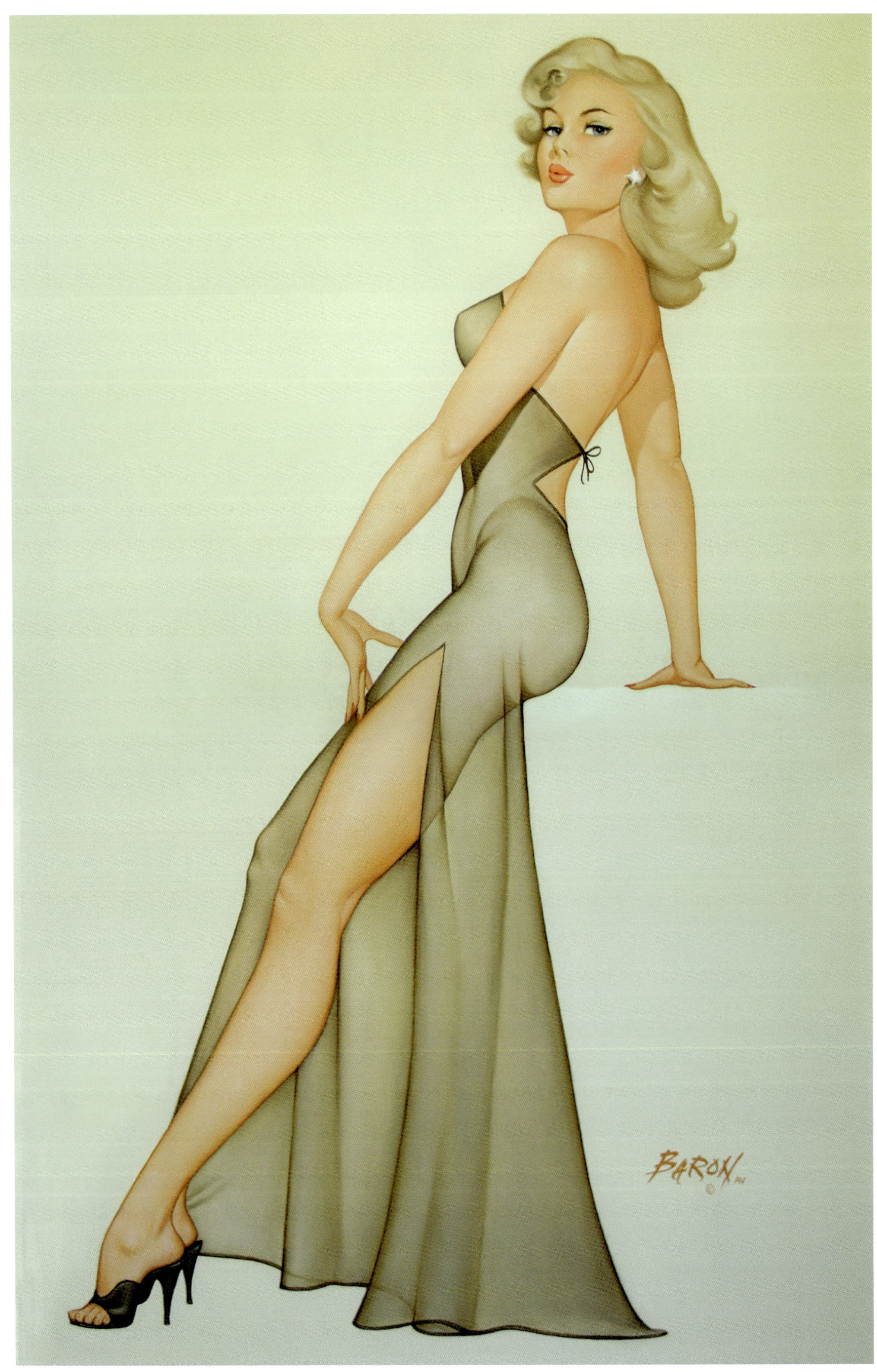
BARON

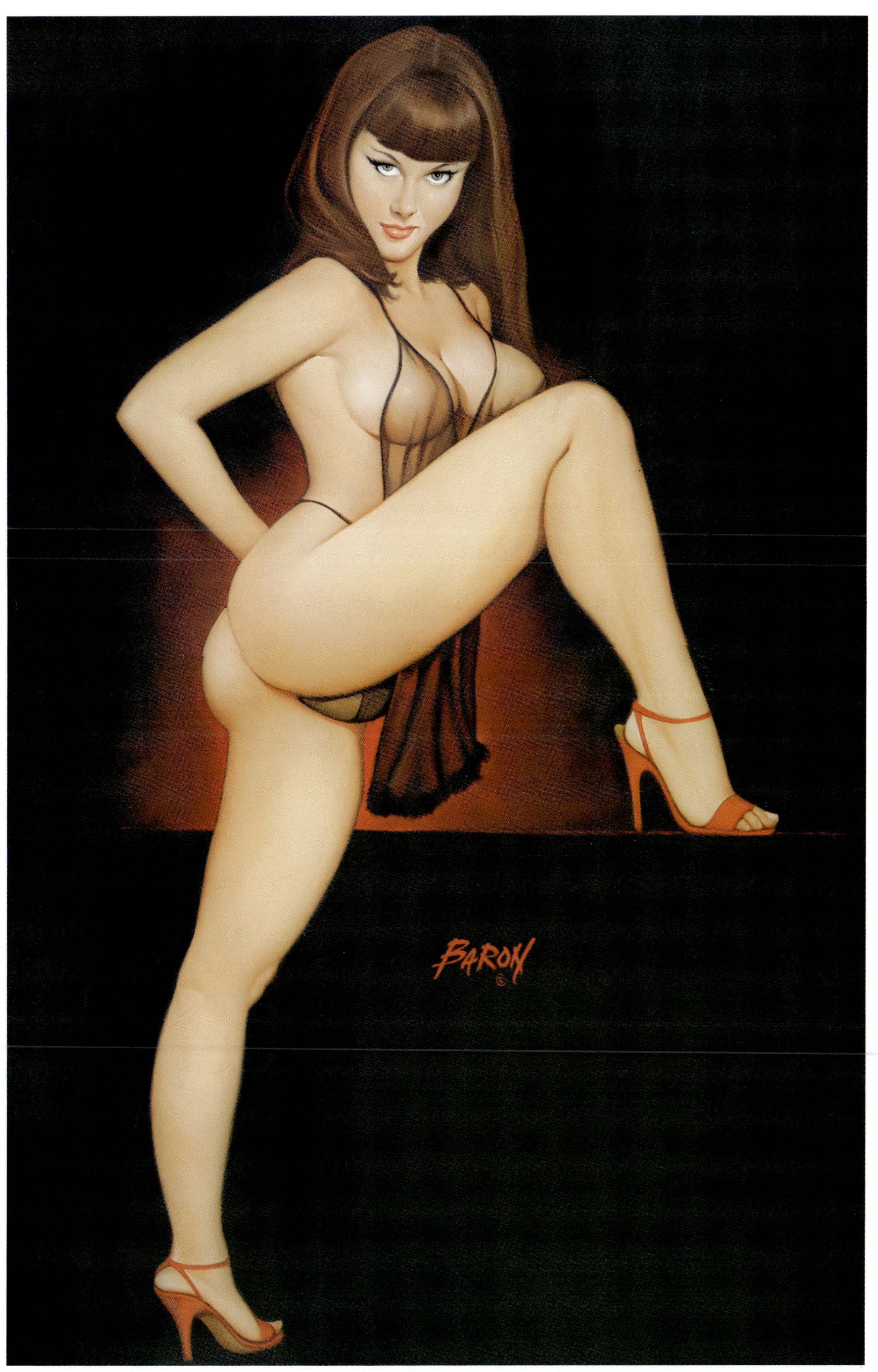
BARON
©

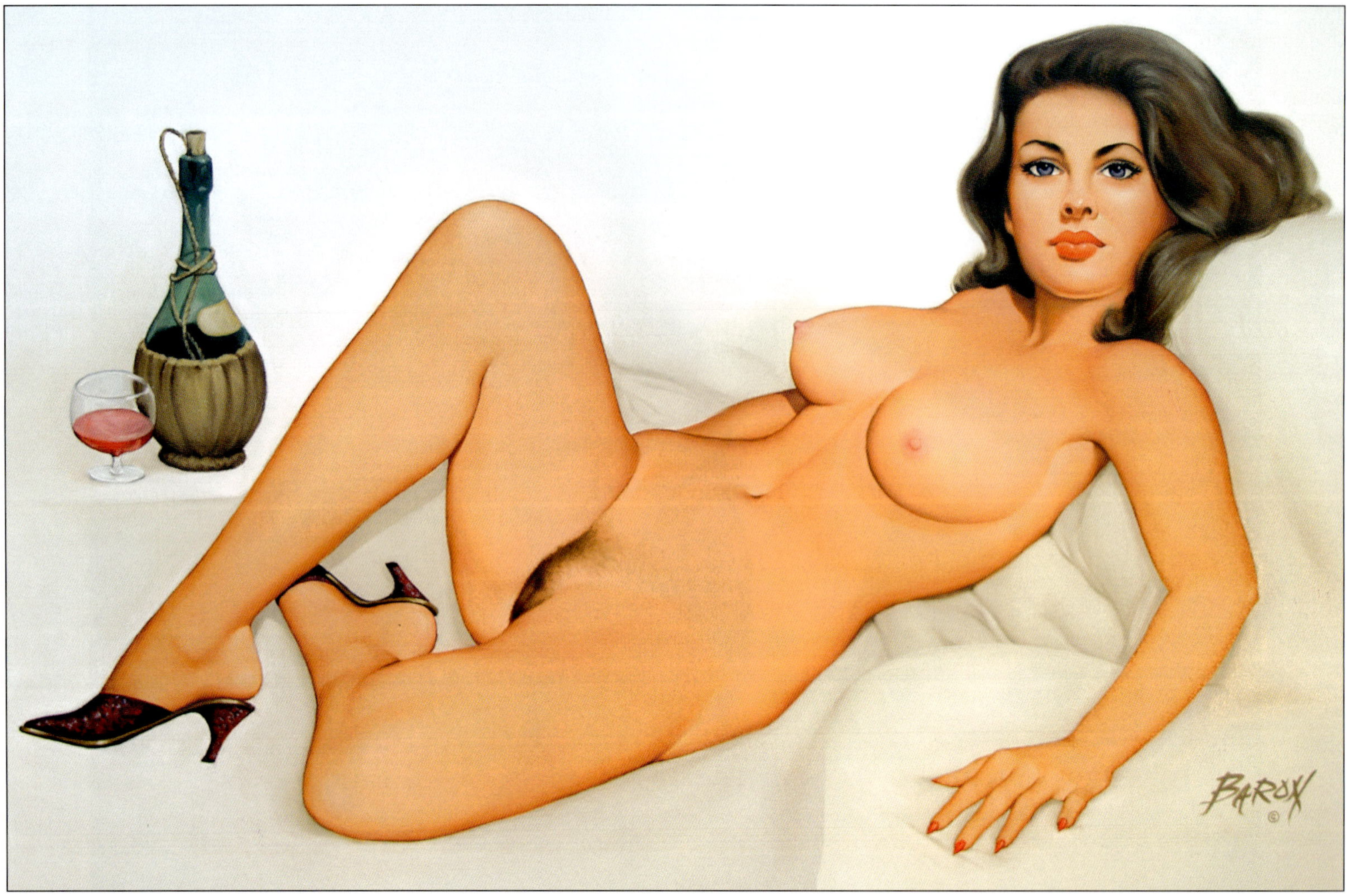

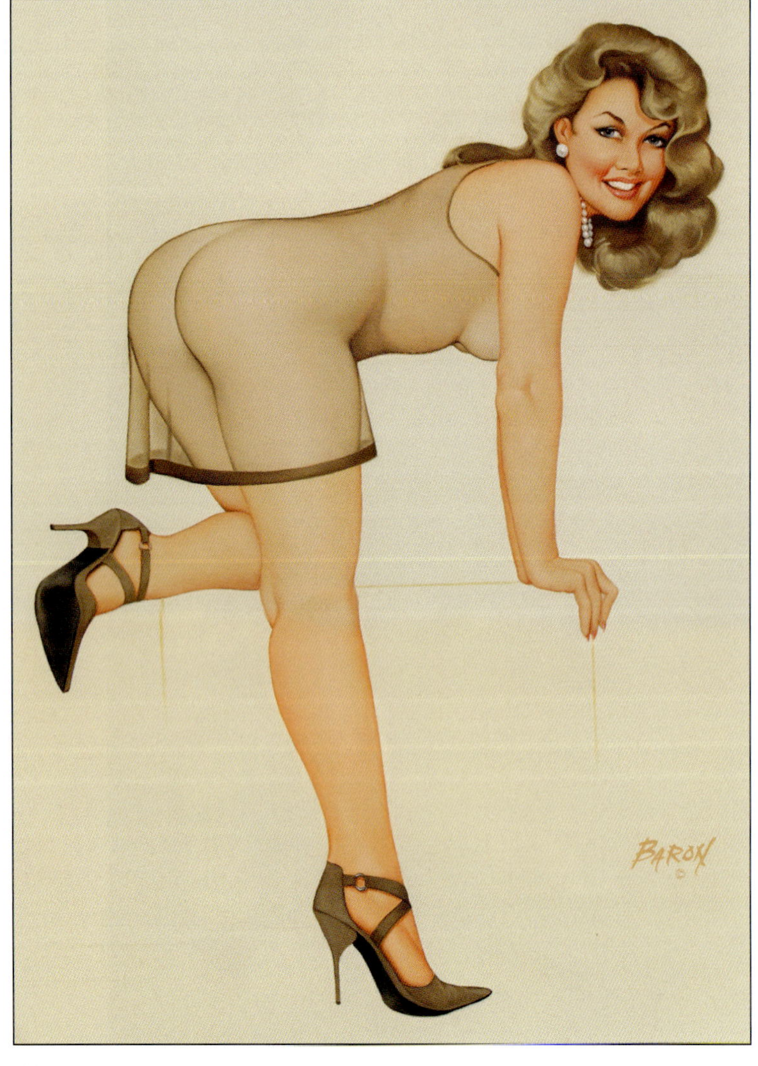
BARON

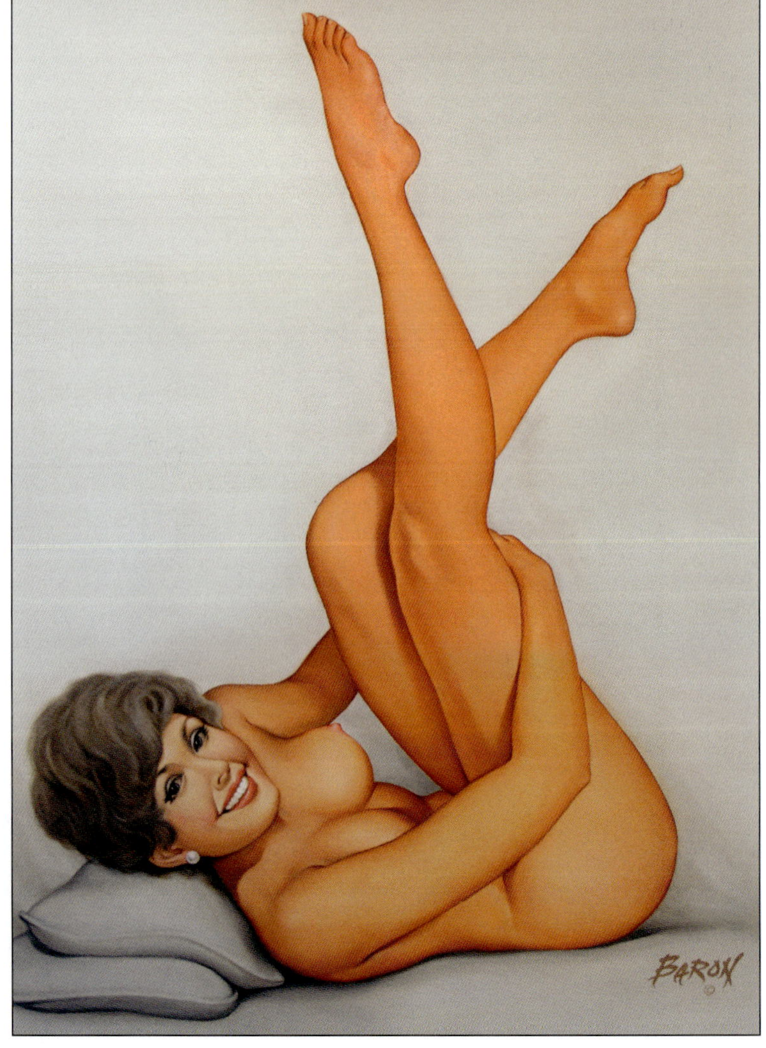
BARON

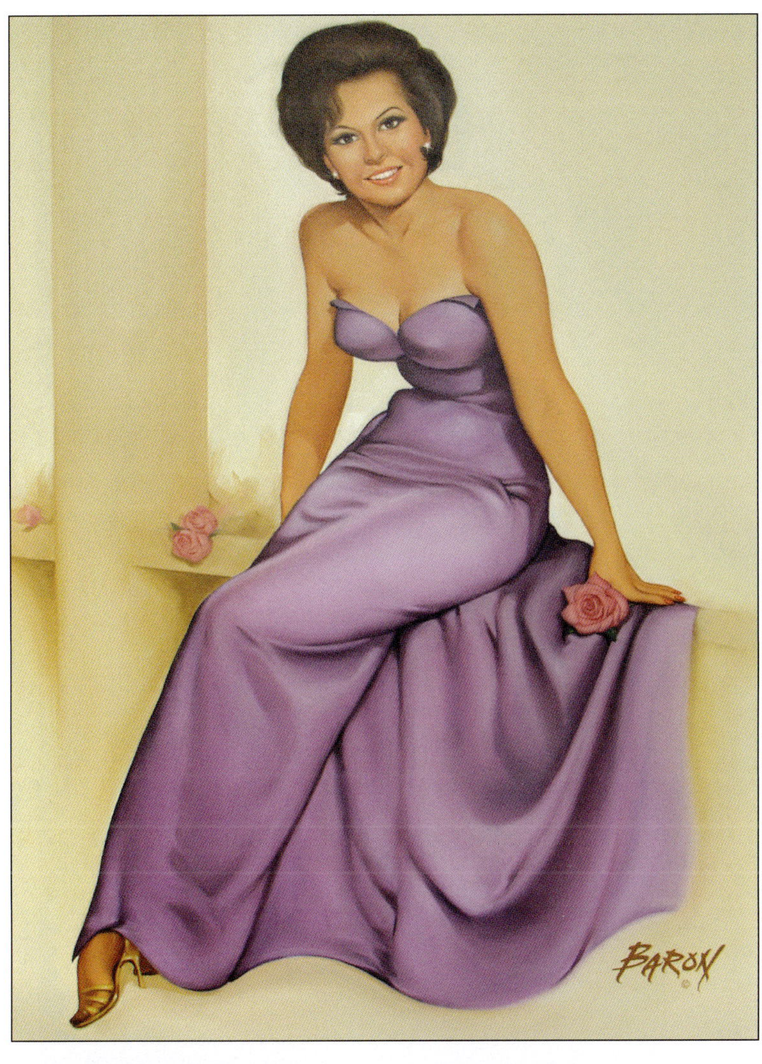
BARON ©

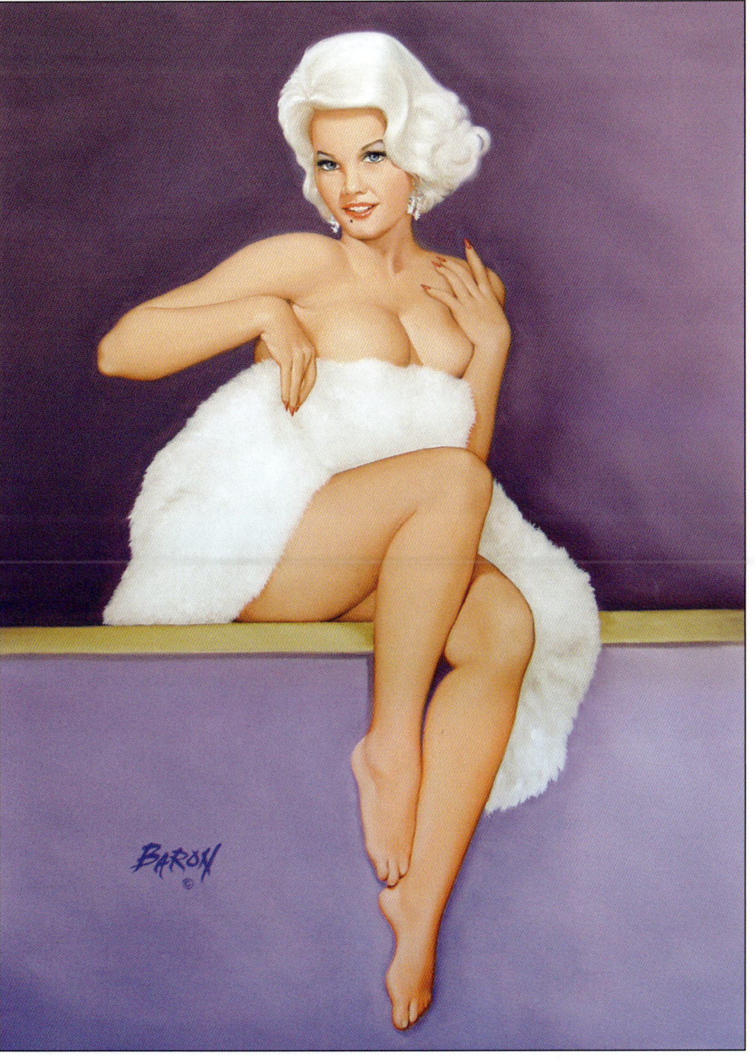
BARON ©

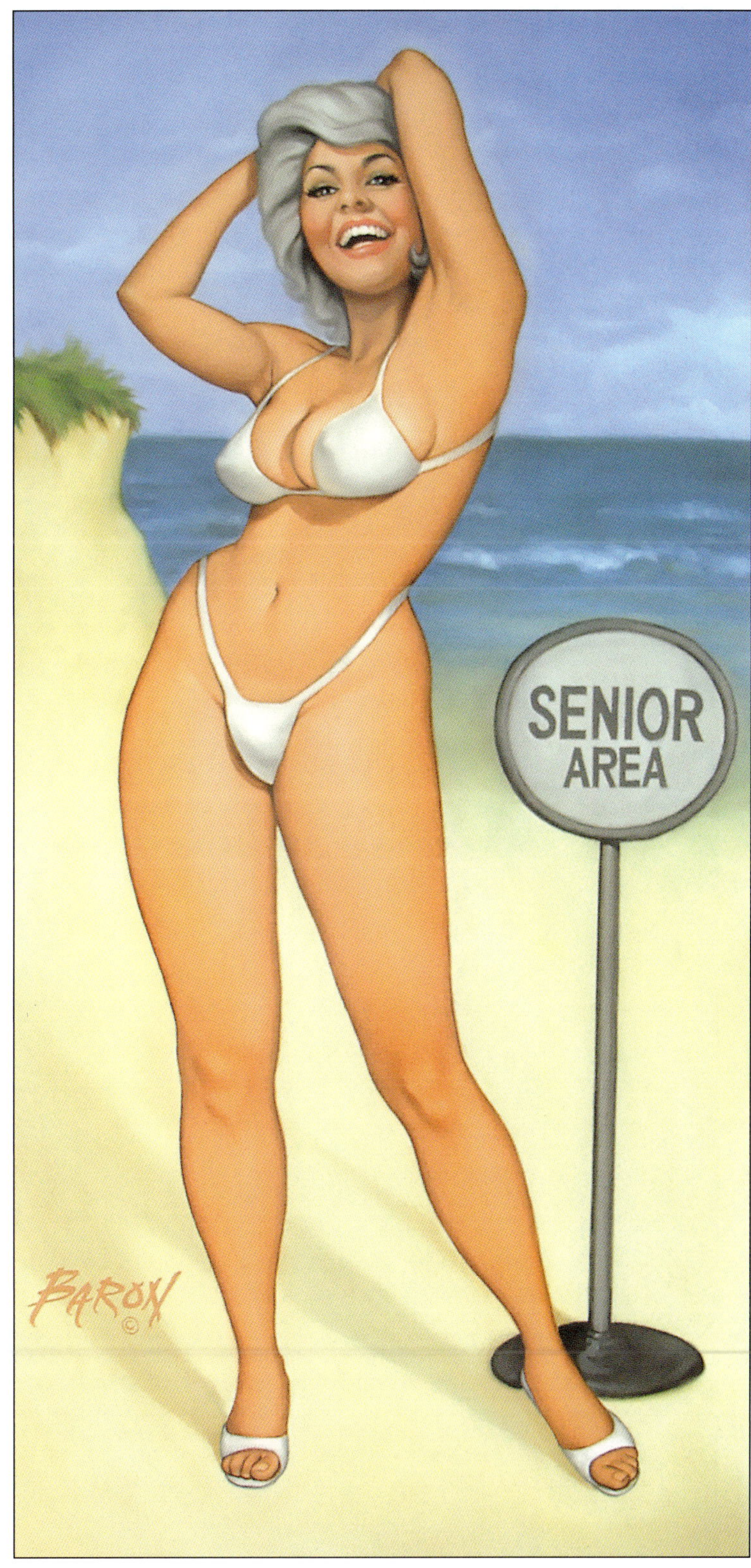
SENIOR
AREA
BARON ©

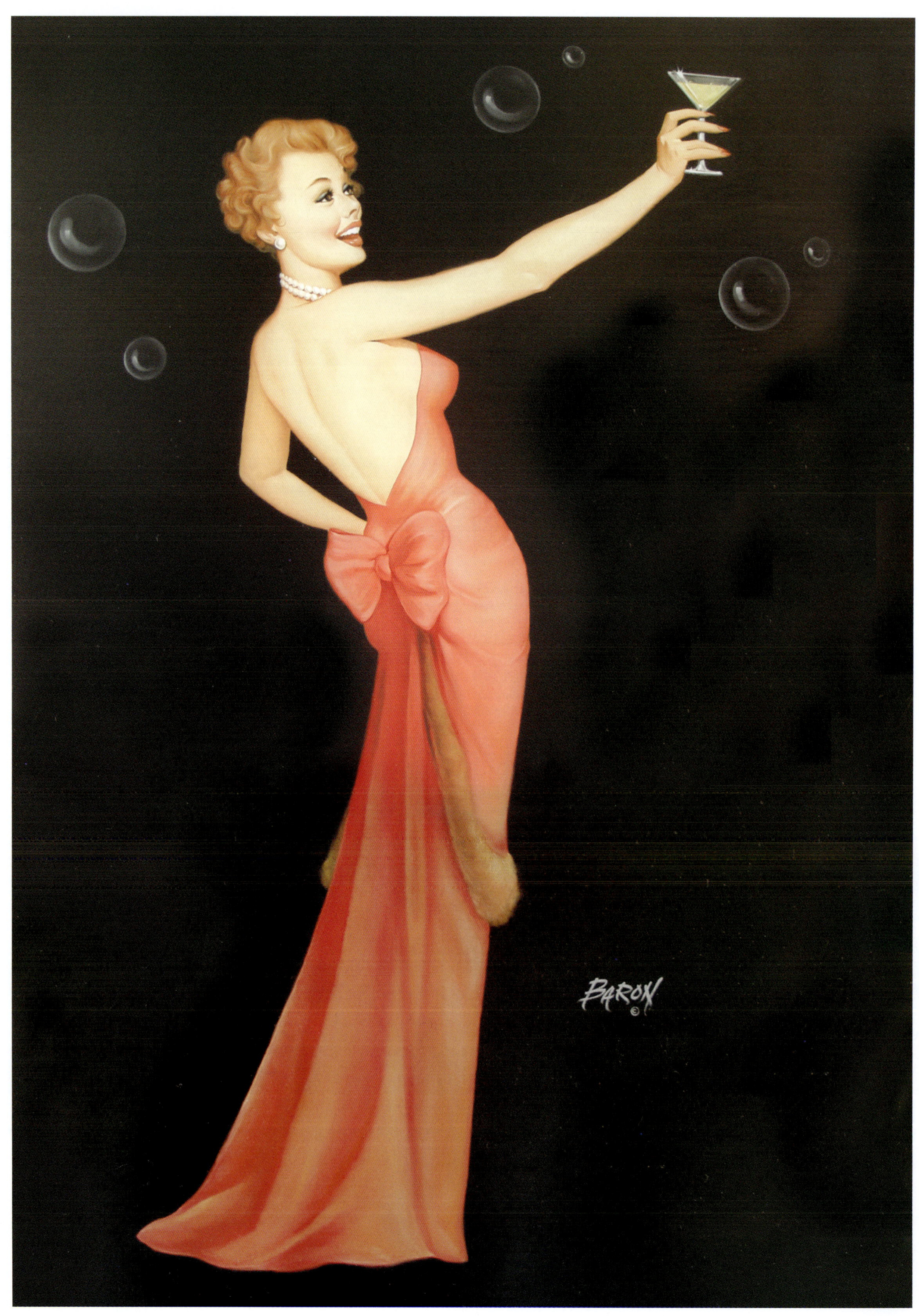
BARON ©

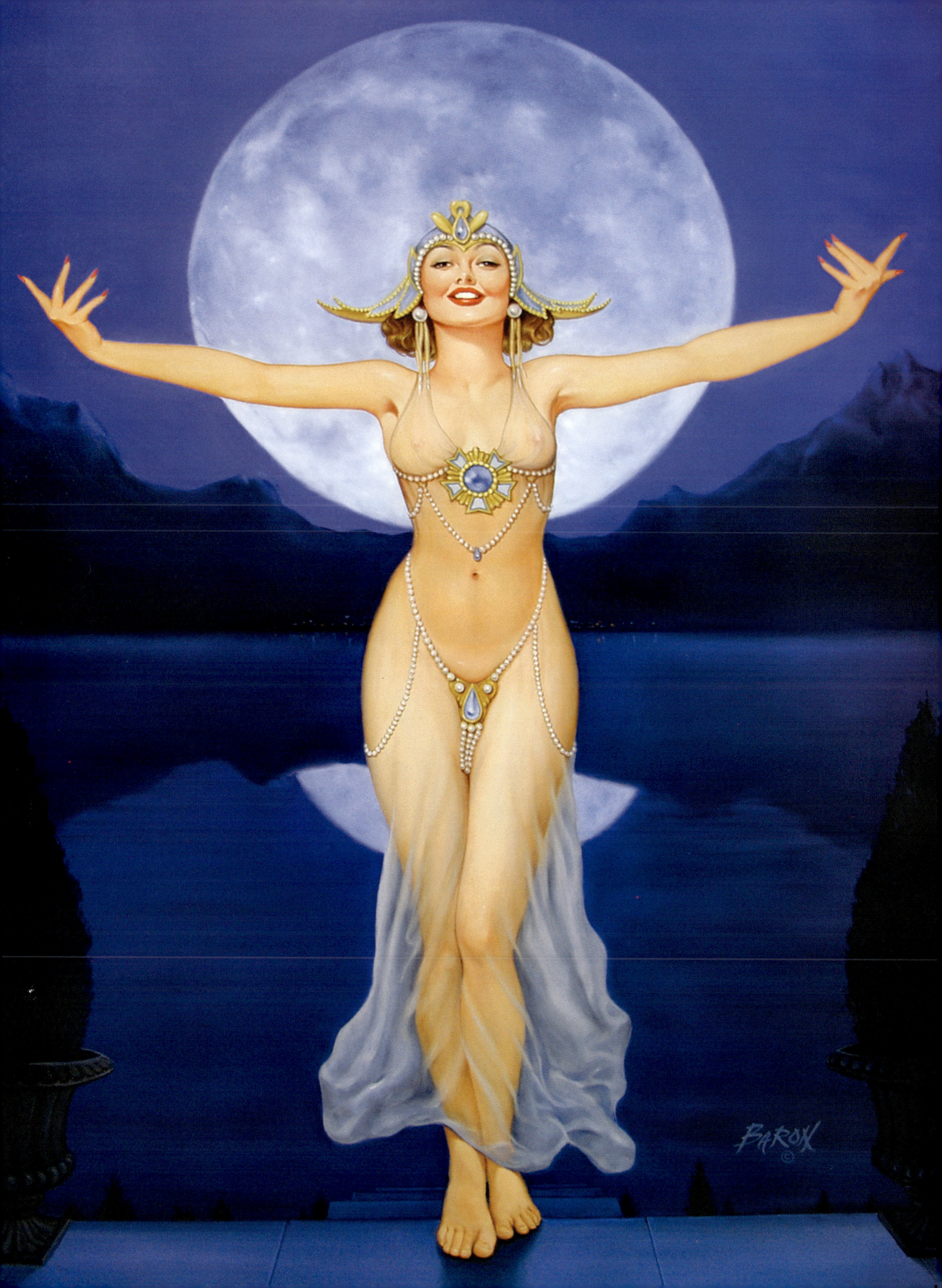
BARON
©

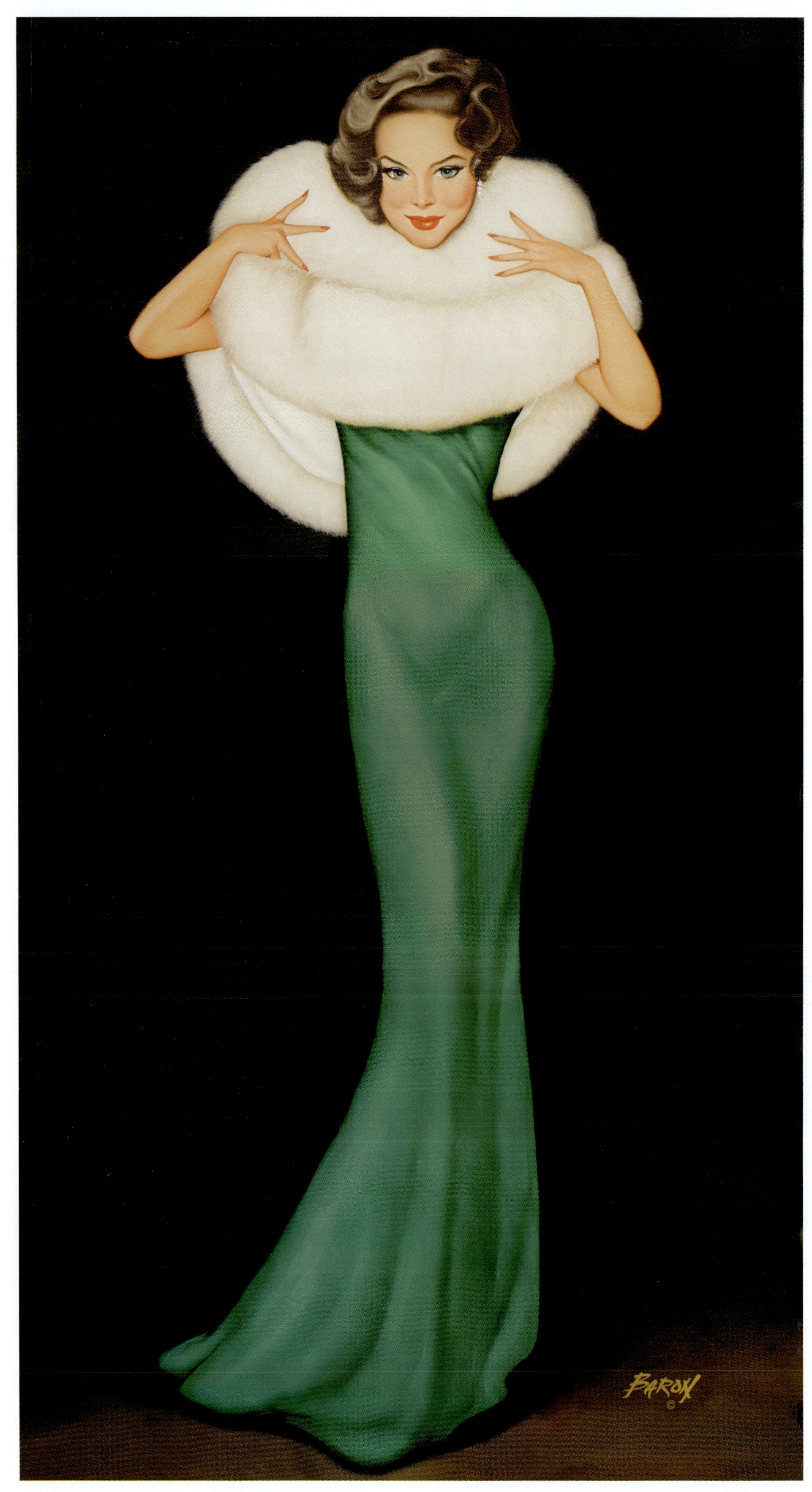
BARON

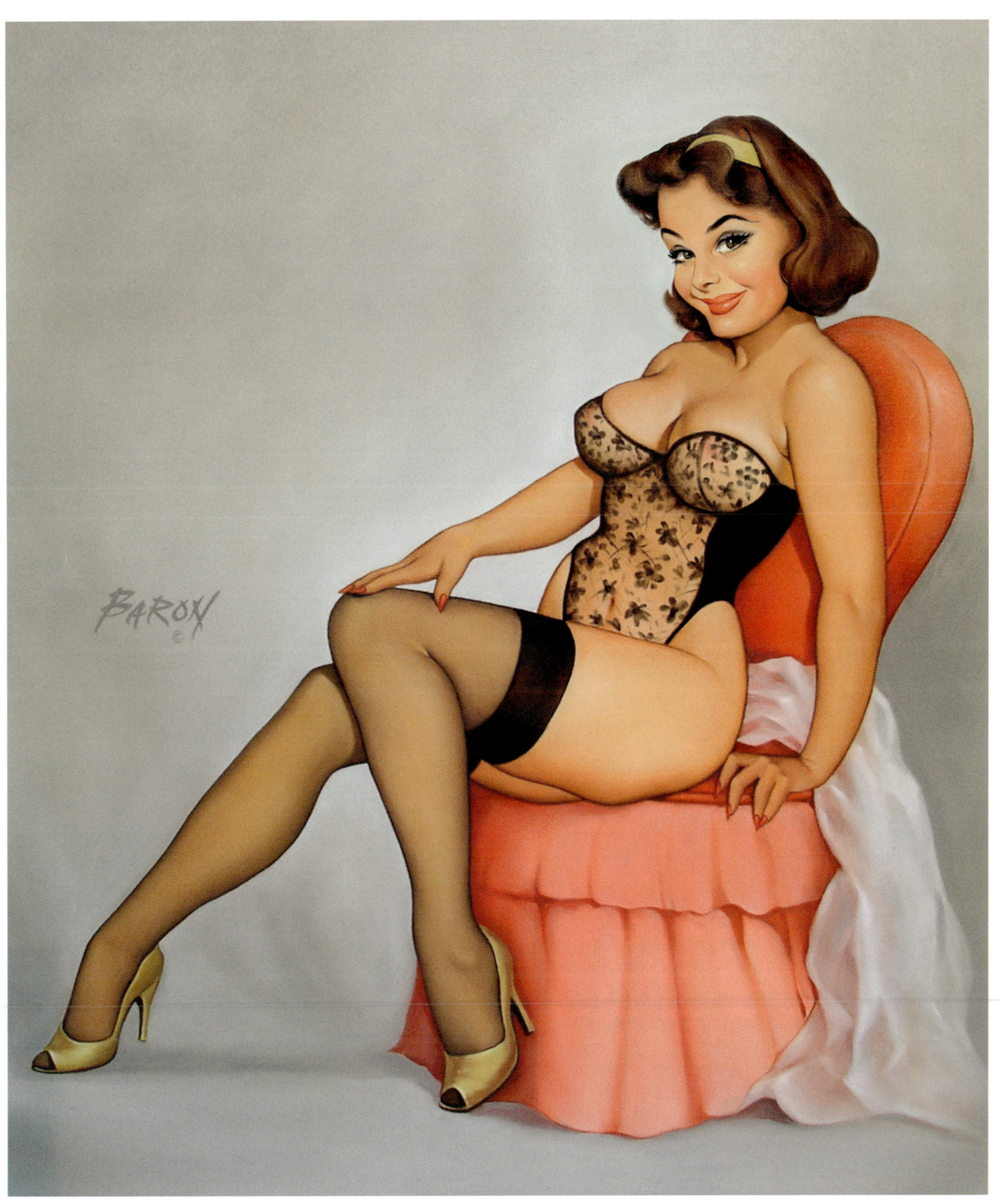
BARON
©

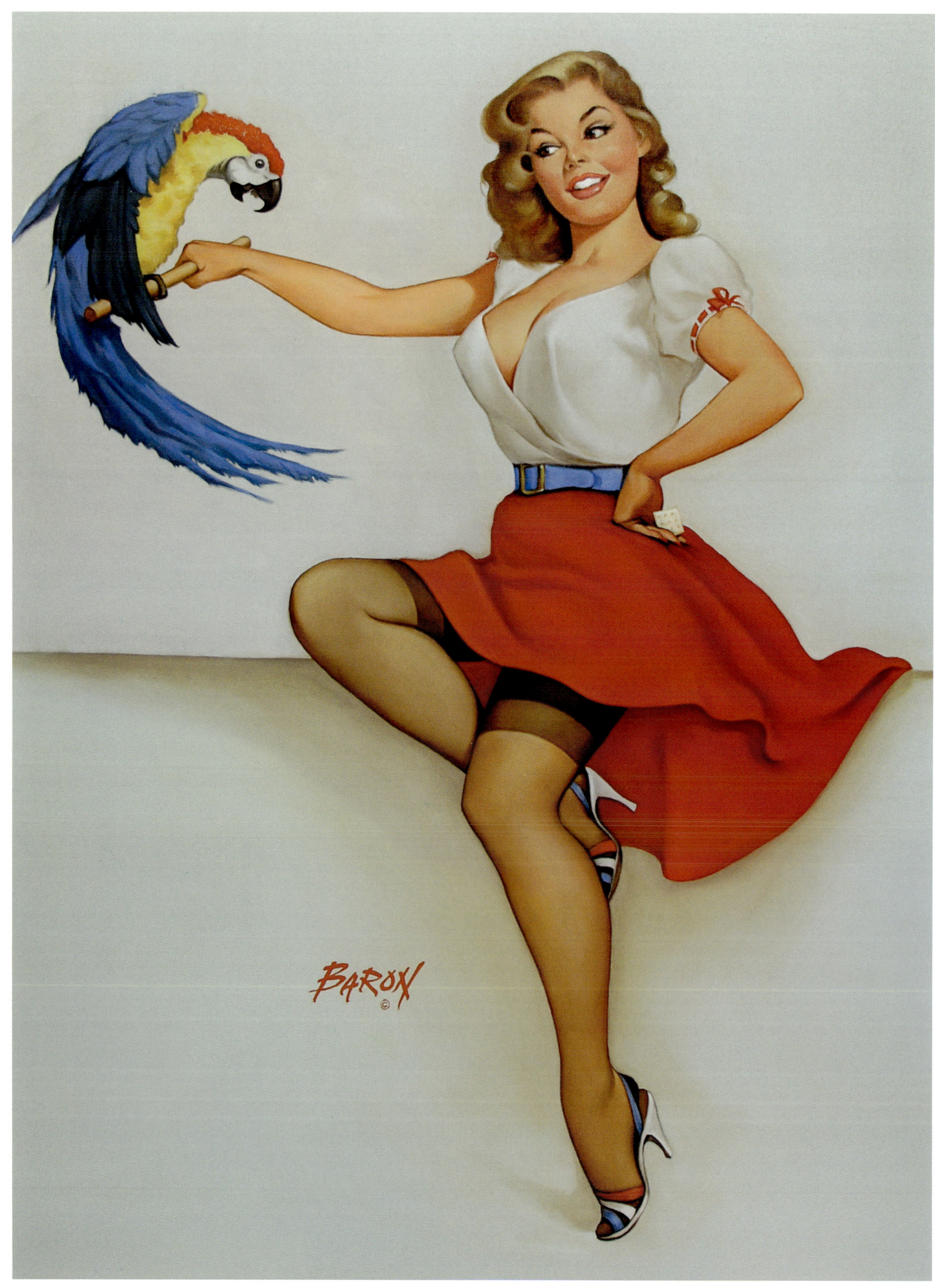
BARON
©

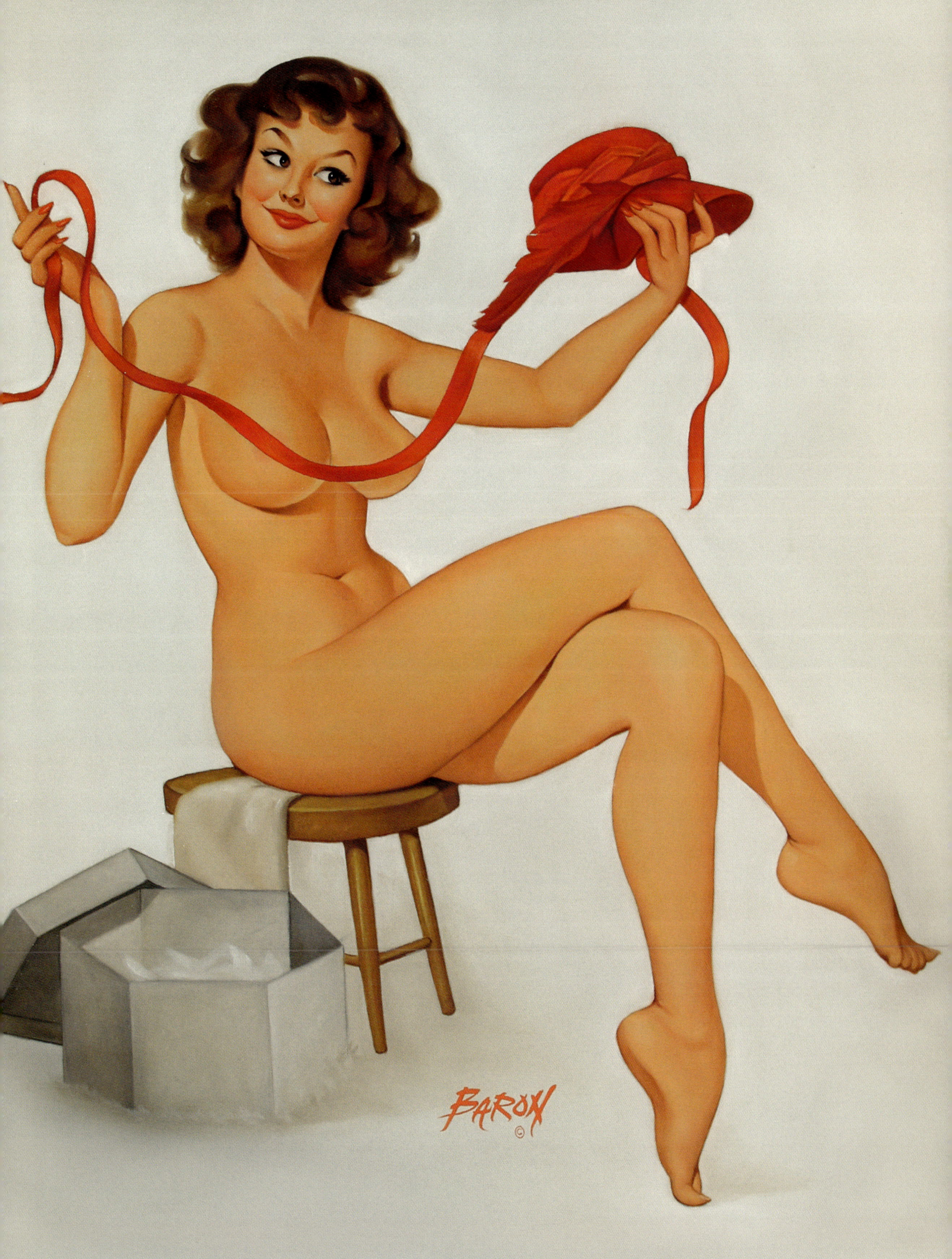
BARON
©

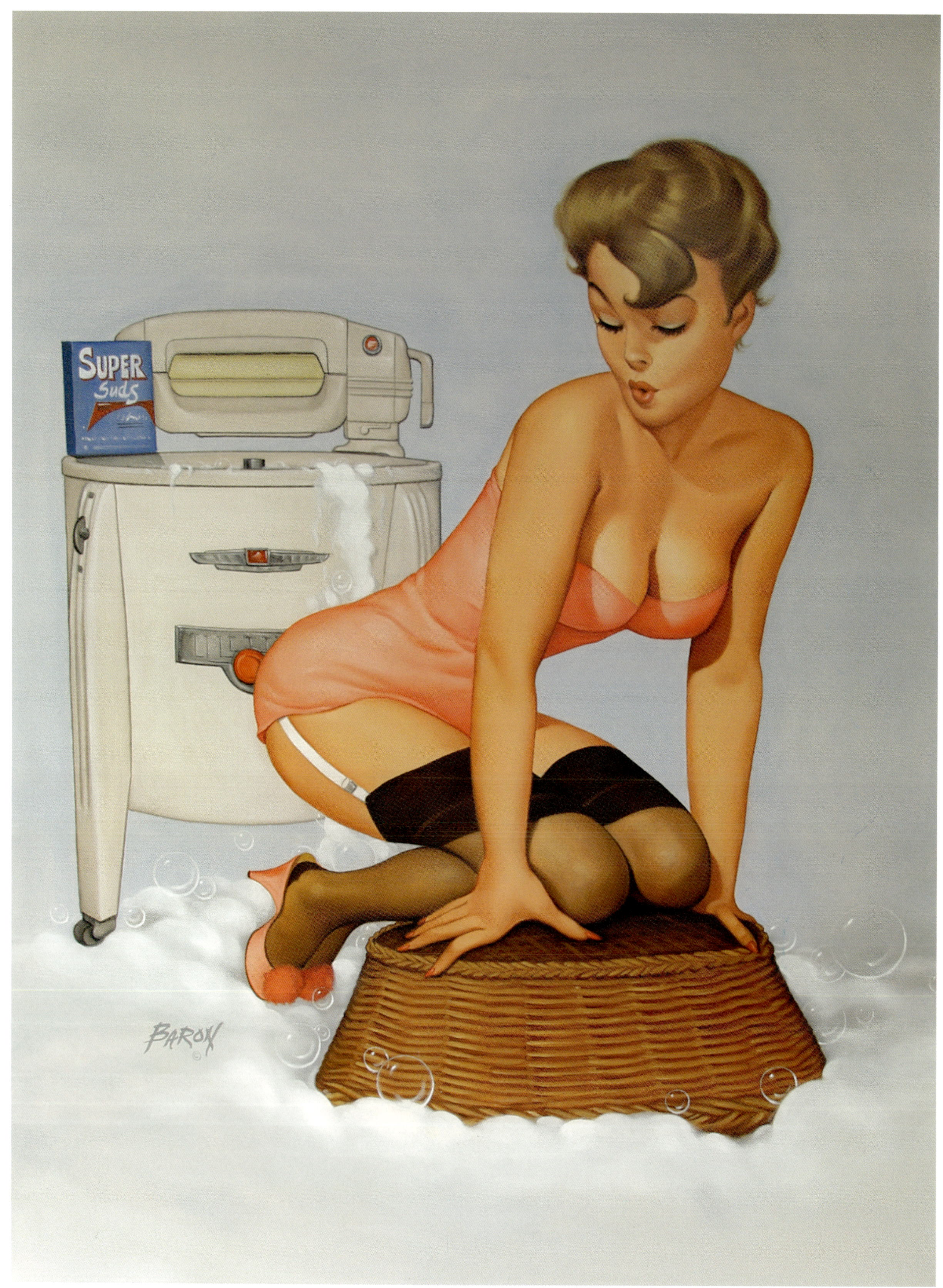
SUPER
Suds
BARON

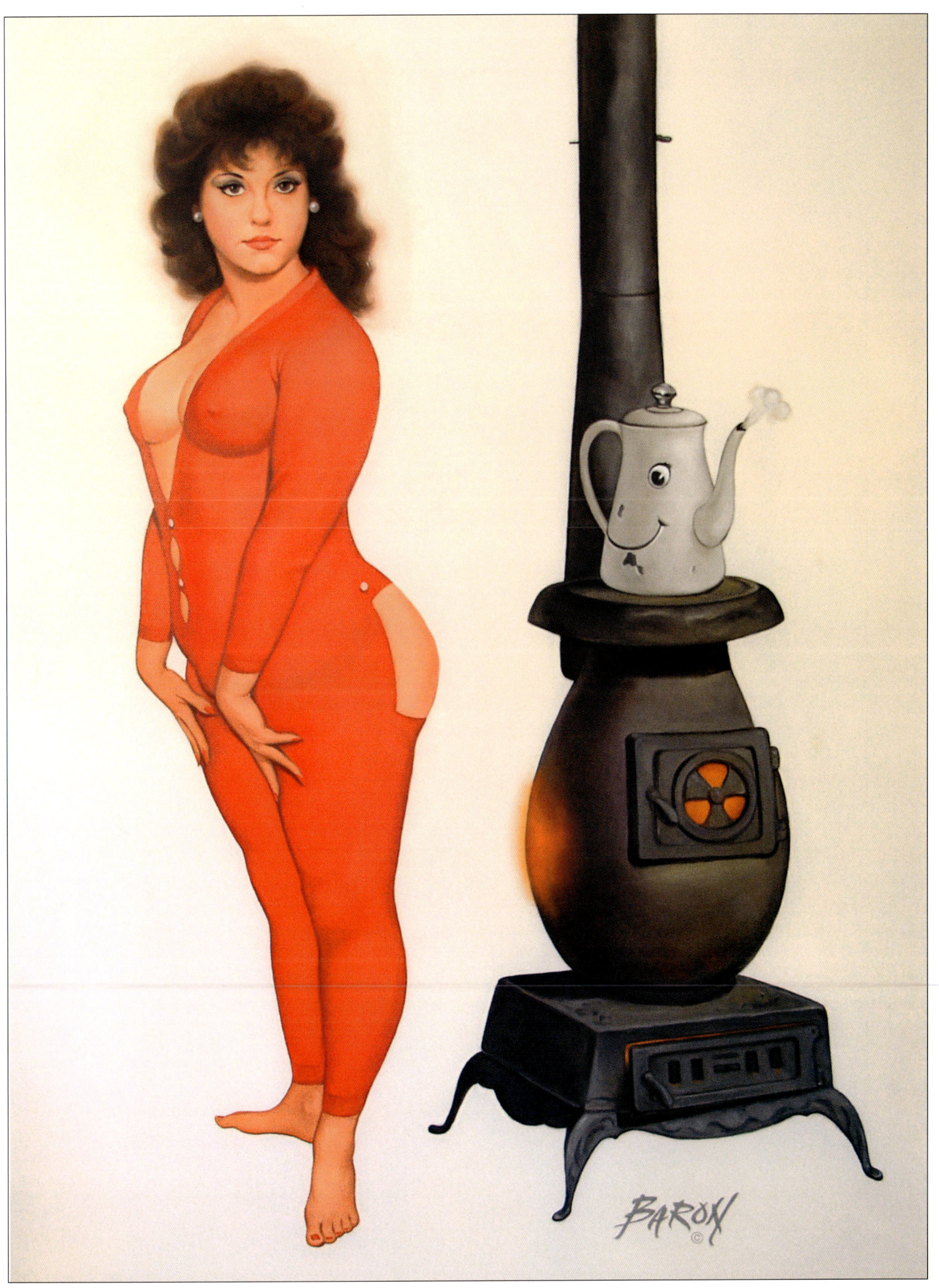
BARON
©

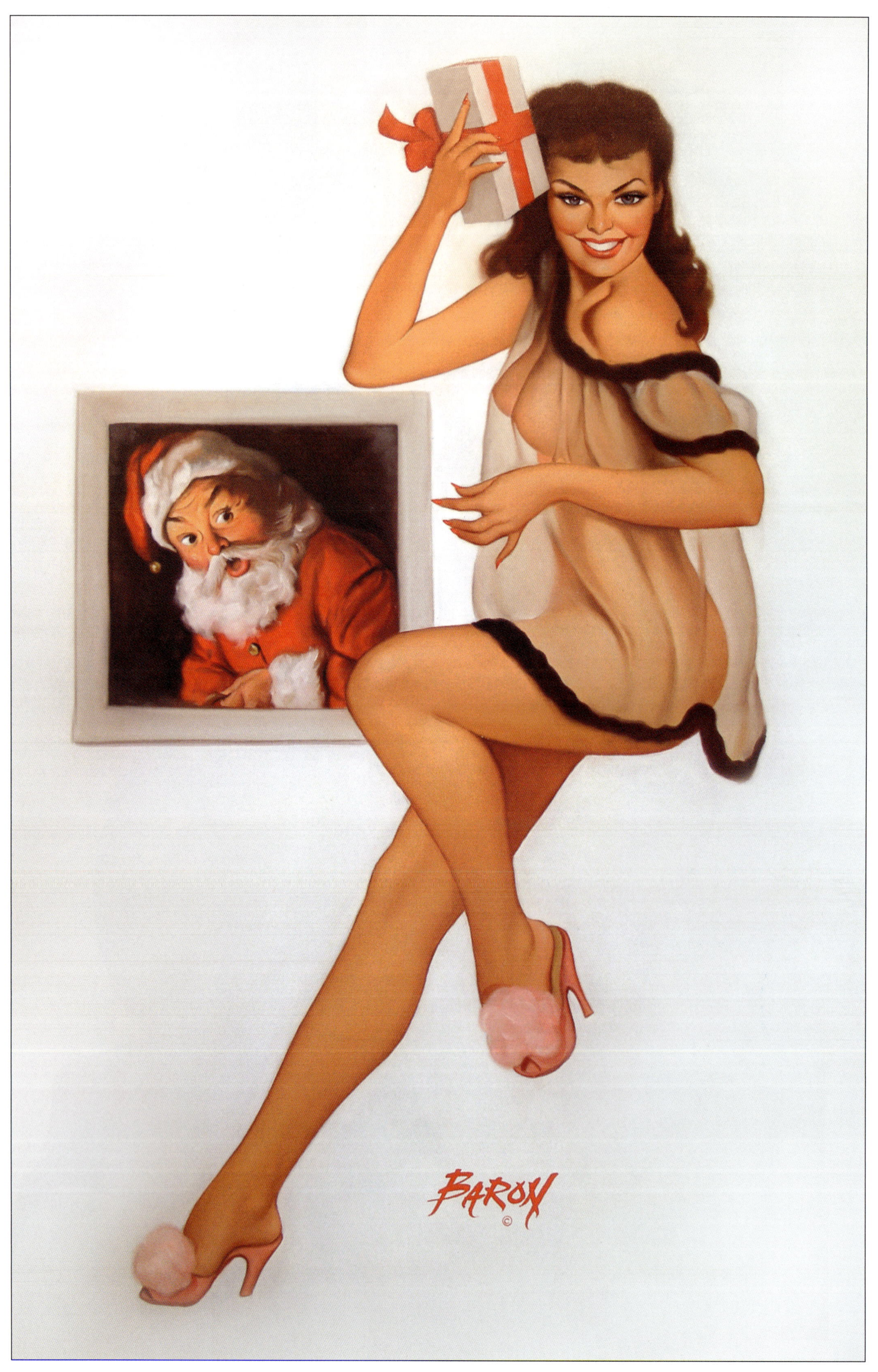
BARON ©

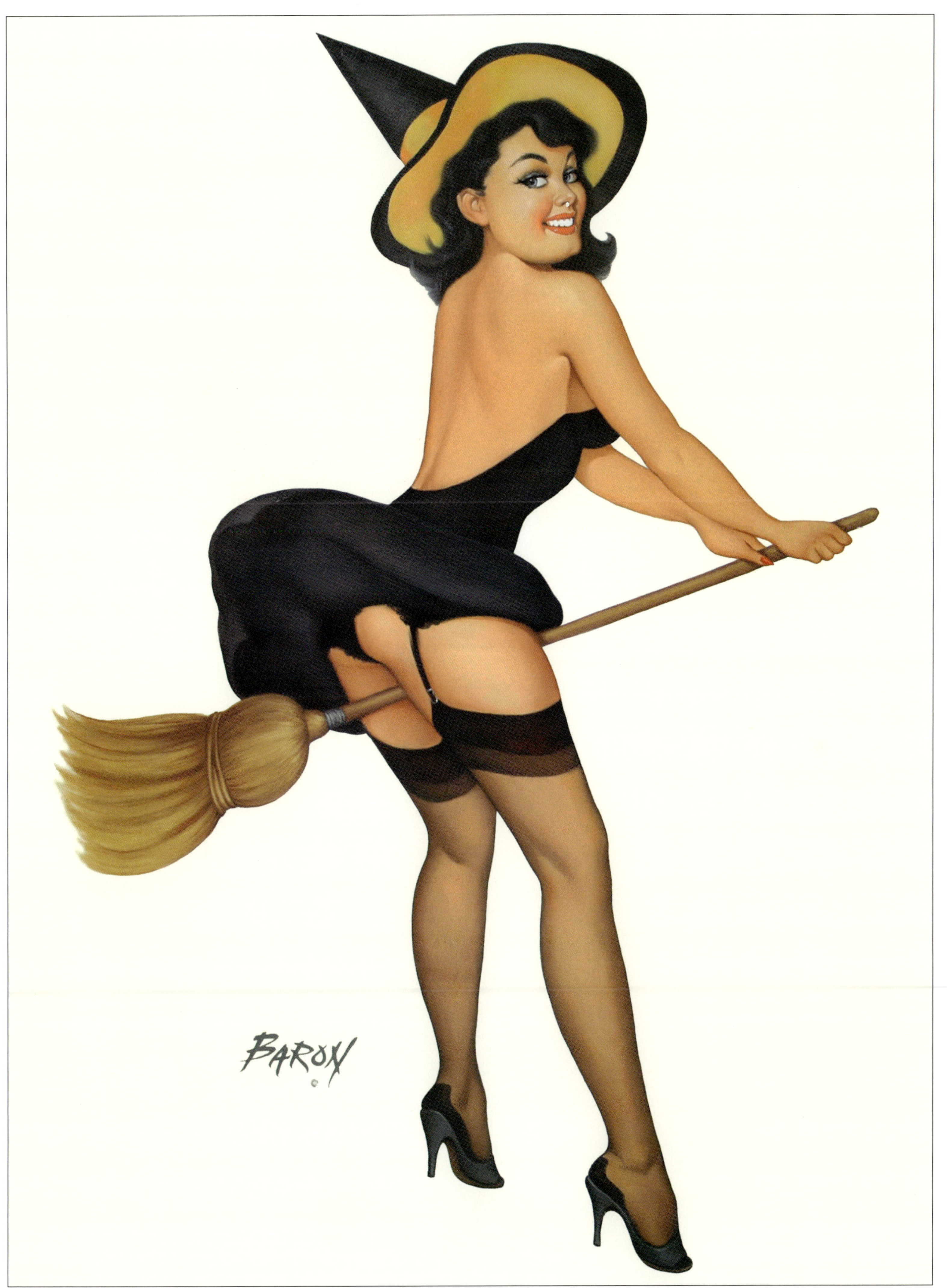
BARON

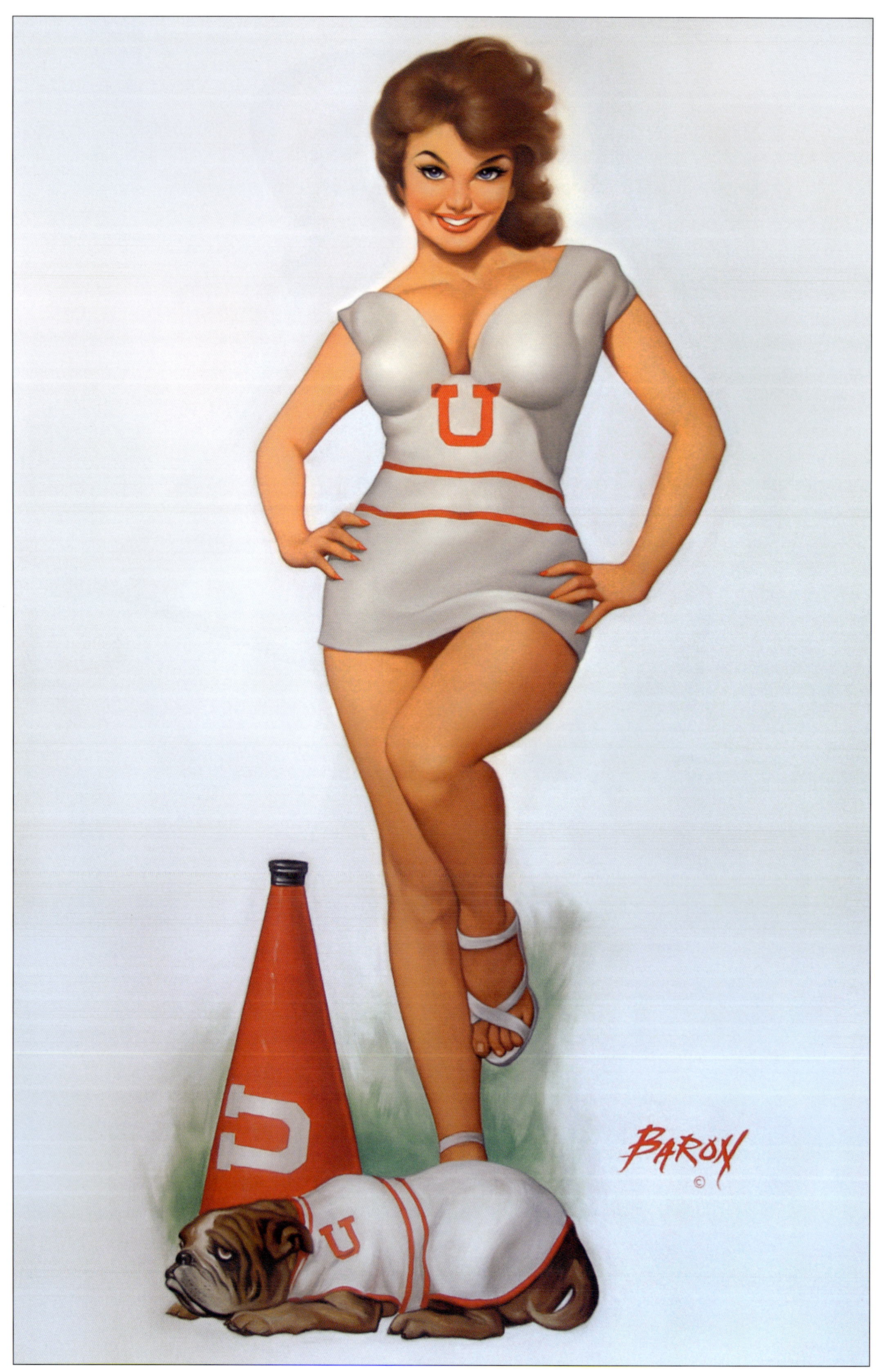
U
U
U
BARON
©

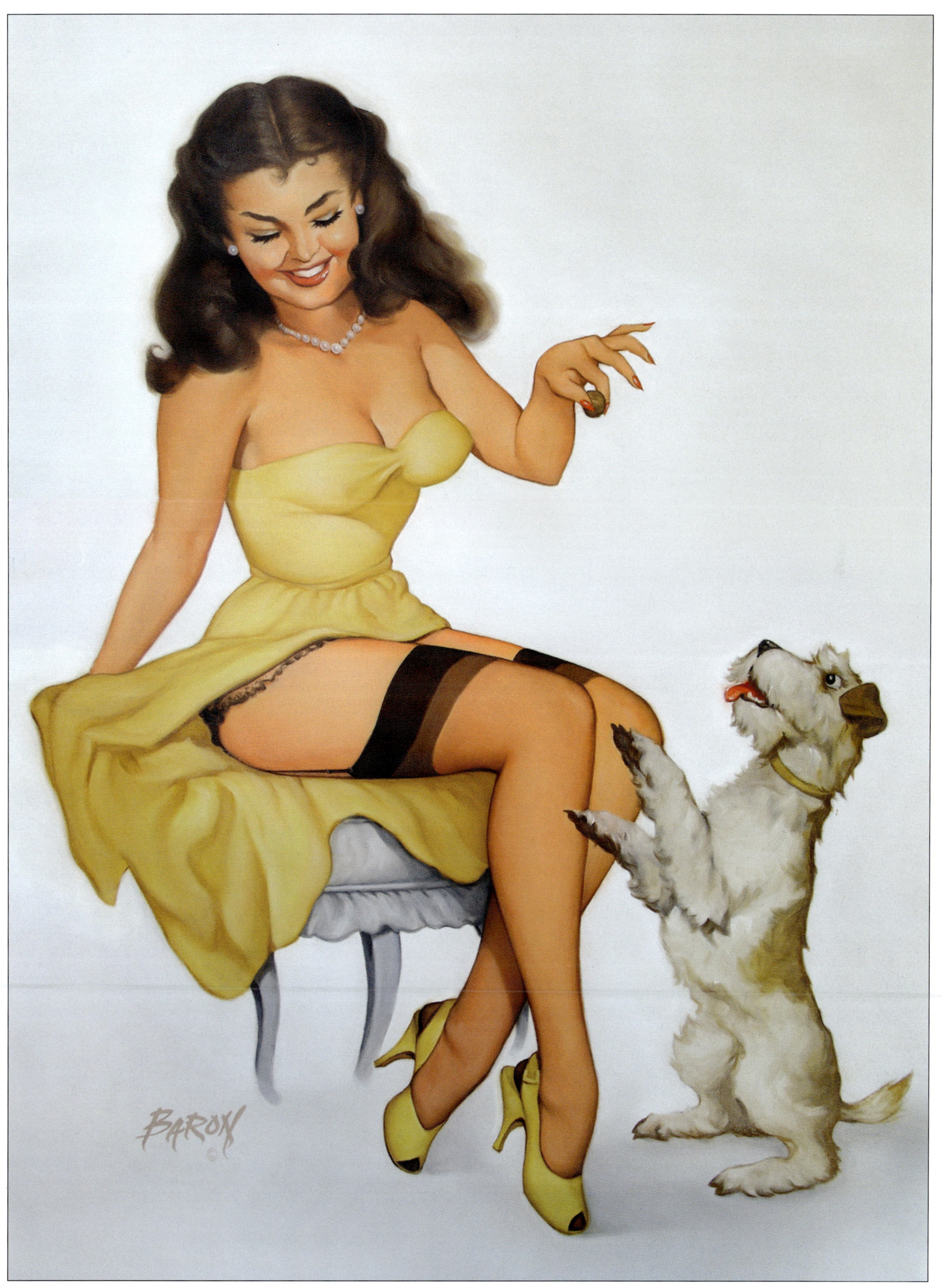
BARON
©

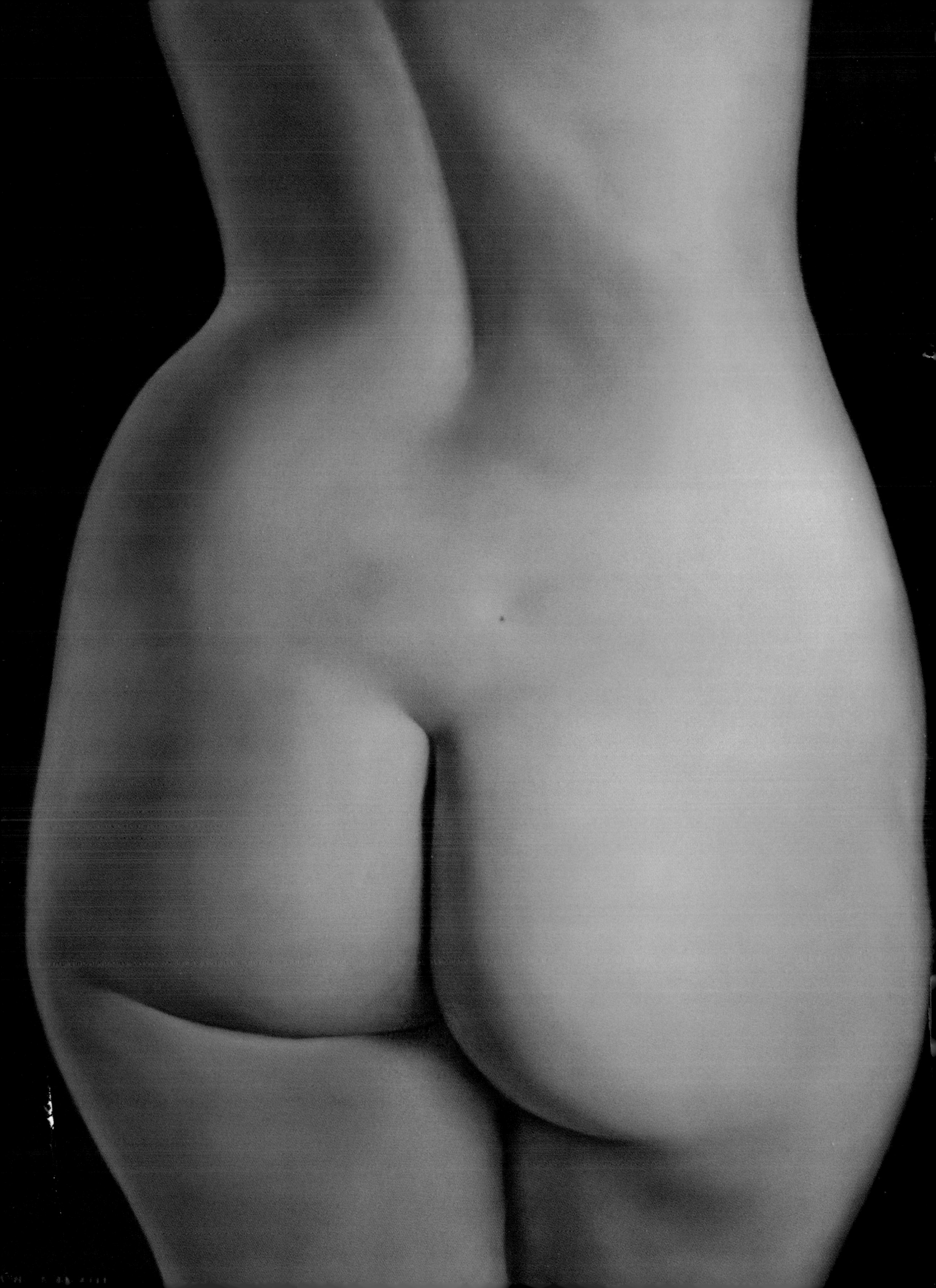